Launch Into Reading Success
Through Phonological Awareness Training

Launch Into Reading Success

Through Phonological Awareness Training

Lorna Bennett
Pamela Ottley

LINKAGE		
Units of Sound	Tapping	Rhyme
Onset and Rime	Segmentation into Syllables	Segmentation into Phonemes
Discrimination	Pronunciation	Blending Phonemes

LINKAGE (left) · LINKAGE (right) · LINKAGE (bottom)

Order this book online at www.trafford.com
or email orders@trafford.com

Most Trafford titles are also available at major online book retailers.

Print information available on the last page.

ISBN: 978-1-6987-0413-5 (sc)
ISBN: 978-1-6987-0411-1 (e)

Library of Congress Control Number: 2020922689

Trafford rev. 11/23/2020

www.trafford.com
North America & international
toll-free: 844-688-6899 (USA & Canada)
fax: 812 355 4082

Contents

INTRODUCTION

Tell me, I'll forget. Show me, and I may remember. But involve me and I'll understand.
—Asian Proberb

FEATURES

Launch into Reading Success Through Phonological Awareness Training offers classroom and learning assistance teachers an **auditory training program** to use with students after initial screening.

This program has been designed by educational psychologists who wish to **transfer research conclusions into educational practice**.

It is particularly useful for teachers working with **kindergarten children at risk of reading delay**; however, it is not limited to this group.

The Nine Sections

- provide **66 activity lessons** for the teacher,

- are sequentially developed and provide a very clear and rich amount of practice at each stage,

- contain stated **learning outcomes and resources** necessary to implement the program,

- give special attention to **pronunciation and explicit linkage**, and

- are very **activity oriented**.

The Student Record Sheets

- offer a way to track progress over time,

- provide teachers with individual and group record forms (see the Appendix), and

- pinpoint the areas where a child needs more help and the specific type of help needed.

This teacher-friendly program requires only minimal extra adult time, which may often be acquired through the use of teacher assistants and/or parents under the teacher's supervision.

RATIONALE

▶ **Phonological awareness is conscious access to the sound structure of words.**

There is widespread agreement that phonological awareness is critical to reading success (Adams, 1990; Blachman, 1994; Hatcher, Hulme, & Ellis, 1994; Torgesen, Wagner, & Rashotte, 1994). Many research studies indicate that approximately 20% to 25% of children do not easily link sounds and letter symbols, and 7% to 10% of children have substantial difficulty and need a comprehensive program involving a great deal of practice. These two groups are the children who need phonological awareness training.

It is now possible to screen all children to determine which children have such low levels of phonological awareness and are at risk of failure. Their training should involve a program so carefully sequenced that

- all possible stages are included, beginning with single words as units of sound and concluding with linkage;

- the sequence of the stages is designed logically; and

- points of breakdown become clear through the systematic assessment of progress.

If these children are not identified and trained, years of unnecessary frustration and failure can result. Research suggests that if there is no intervention until the later years (e.g., by age 9), more than three quarters of the 20% to 25% group will continue to have problems at the high school level.

Teachers who use an early screening method to detect those children at risk of reading delay/failure and use *Launch Into Reading Success* as an intervention will benefit from knowing that the research overwhelmingly concludes that reading success or failure is linked to the development of phonological awareness skills. It will be seen as a powerful tool within a continuum of help for children with mild to severe indicators of literacy problems.

PHONOLOGICAL AWARENESS—A SEQUENCE

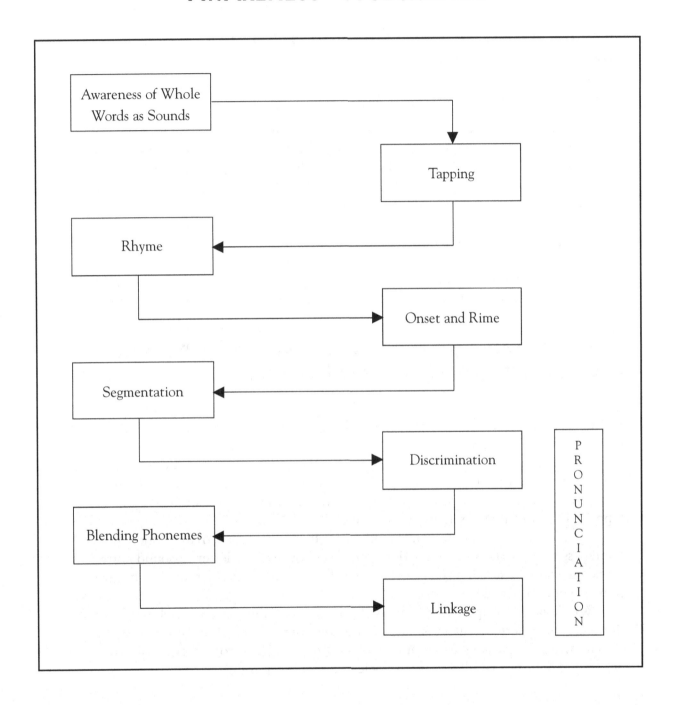

VITAL ANSWERS
TO VITAL QUESTIONS

How Do We Know Which Children Need Phonological Awareness Training?

Screening tests (e.g., *Test of Phonological Awareness* (Torgesen & Bryant, 1994), *Dyslexia Early Screening Test* (Nicholson & Fawcett, 1996), *Phonological Abilities Test* (Hulme, Muter, & Snowling, 1997) measure the responses of children to a carefully designed range of phonological awareness tasks. Several are administered one-on-one, taking between 20 and 30 minutes per child. Others allow group administration, which is faster but may be slightly less reliable. Usually students scoring below the 25th percentile will benefit from early intervention.

These tests have been successful in finding at least 80% of children at risk of reading difficulty, many of whom would not be selected in other ways. However, experienced teachers who have concerns about other children are urged to include them in the intervention group.

The "assessment over time" facility of this program will give useful information.

How Is Phonological Awareness Different from Phonics and How Is it Related to Whole Language?

This training stands outside the "Phonics Versus Whole Language" debate. Phonological awareness is different from phonic skills, and it is very important to understand the difference between the two processes.

Phonological awareness training aims to give children conscious access to the sounds within words. It is primarily auditory training and is very activity oriented. Sounds of words are introduced and reinforced utilizing a variety of strategies such as tapping, clapping, rhyme schemes, games, etc.

Phonic instruction, however, is a different stage and process than phonological awareness training. Phonic instruction provides knowledge of letter-to-sound correspondence so that children can encode and decode; this strategy tends to involve some paper-and-pencil exercises.

Whole language approaches are essential. Children always need a rich source of literature in supported situations, such as looking, sharing, paired reading, and being read to, which emphasizes the meaning of language as opposed to its form. This strategy should continue parallel to phonological awareness training.

Where and When Should it Be Done?

Launch Into Reading Success will remain great fun as a daily short activity! The authors believe that the best place to work is a quiet corner of the classroom. This prevents any message that the selected group is labeled or has special needs.

The time of day will be set mainly by the practicalities facing the teacher. However, it would be unwise to do this program toward the end of the afternoon, when children are tired.

What Do I Say to Parents?

"Phonological awareness training, when provided at an early age, will help your child be better prepared for reading and spelling. This training will help your child to develop better listening skills and to hear distinctly the sounds within spoken words."

How Does it Fit with the Curriculum?

Launch Into Reading Success fits perfectly with the important kindergarten curriculum aims of teaching good listening skills, exploring all aspects of spoken language, and giving experience with the form of language (as opposed to the meaning of language). This is probably a relatively neglected aspect in the homes of preschool children today.

There is, therefore, no stigma attached to a group of children who do a little more of this work because their levels of phonological awareness are not as high as those of their peers.

Sometimes extra reading programs are used when there are early signs of delay or difficulty. One example of this is the Reading Recovery Program (Clay, 1991). Such a program would be entirely complementary to early phonological awareness training because fluency and supported access to meaning must be continued throughout. Such a program would also be enhanced by the valuable basis provided by phonological awareness training.

How Does the Program Support the Common Curriculum Framework?

It is relevant to all five general learning outcomes found in the Common Curriculum Framework of British Columbia, Canada. Bear in mind that at-risk children are a subset of all children. It especially relates to general outcome number two which states, "Comprehend and respond personally and critically to literacy and media texts," because a whole group of children will be unable to successfully go ahead unless they have sound/structure awareness as the first step in a continuum of help.

Launch Into Reading Success is directly linked to *The Common Curriculum Framework for English Language Arts, Kindergarten to Grade 12,* in the following ways:

- makes connections between oral language, texts, and personal experiences

- recognizes that print is organized from top to bottom and left to right

- recognizes that letters present sounds
- participates in shared listening
- demonstrates curiosity about and experiments with letters, sounds, words, and word patterns
- retells ideas to clarify meaning
- connects sounds with letters in words
- contributes to group activities using rhymes, rhythms, symbols, and pictures to create and celebrate
- participates in group activities

Fluent expressive ability in language does not always ensure proficiency with reading. There can be hidden phonological awareness deficits which will prevent literacy development.

Awareness of the speech sound structure is the first step in becoming a successful reader.

How Do I Use the Program?

View this program as an important segment to dovetail nicely with all the other enjoyable and valuable auditory training elements (e.g., enjoying rhymes) that you use in the form of language at this early educational stage.

Identify a time in the day when this group of children can work with yourself or with a teacher aide or parent volunteer. The session should run for approximately 30 minutes (sometimes a little less, but very rarely more).

The session plans, and the steps outlined, should be followed sequentially.

It is important to keep a record of group and individual progress, using the convenient record sheets (see the Appendix). These sheets can be used to note any difficulties a child may have at an early stage. This will become a valuable assessment for future teaching and for enlisting some parental support if necessary.

How Much Time Is Involved?

Launch Into Reading Success requires a maximum of 30 minutes daily for each lesson.

You can teach the group while the rest of the class is occupied and supervised by another staff member. More often the lessons will be done by a teacher aide or parent volunteer who is working closely under your supervision.

Obviously there will be unusual days when the whole timetable changes and the lessons cannot be done at all. However, try as much as possible to maintain consistent daily input because the program was designed in this manner. Longer sessions, twice a week, are not advised.

Why Should Phonological Awareness Training Be Done in Kindergarten?

Early intervention has been shown to produce significantly better progress in reading (Bryant & Bradley, 1985).

Do I Need Special Training?

There is no special training needed to begin work with children using *Launch Into Reading Success* because each activity is carefully scripted. However, it is important to assemble the materials needed before each session.

What Is Linkage?

Researchers Byrne and Fielding-Barnsley (1990) found that in order for children to understand the alphabetic principle, three components must be in place: Children must be able to isolate phonemes within words, understand that sounds can be common between words, and know that specific sounds can be represented by particular letters. The first two components are not enough. Children need to be explicitly taught to make the link between letters and sounds. When children are provided with reading and phonological awareness training (but neither is linked), how to make the connection is left to the child; this is non-explicit linkage. When the child is shown how to connect the three components, explicit linkage has occurred. The linkage activities in this program represent a way of explicitly introducing sound-symbol connections.

EQUIPMENT LIST

These activities require the sort of materials routinely found in kindergarten and first-grade classrooms. Teachers are extremely busy, and planning time is at a premium. Therefore, everything needed is either within the book, photocopiable from the book, or on the list below.

Manipulatives

counters
colored cubes
plastic letters
blocks
interlocking building toys

Storage Materials

plastic storage bags
(small)

Miscellaneous

hand puppet
mirror
marble
two toy cars
sand tray

General Supplies

paper plate
pencils
crayons
scissors
glue stick or glue
ruler

Percussion Instruments

drumstick
mallet
stick

TERMINOLOGY

Phonology	• The system of (spoken) language which relates meanings and sounds • A study of the sound system of languages • Development of (a child's) speech sounds
Phonological Awareness	• Conscious access to the sound structure of words
Phonemes	• The smallest units of sound that can affect meaning (within a word) • 26 letters but 44 phonemes because of dual usage (e.g., *c* as in *cat* and *c* as in cell), and digraphs (e.g., **shi***p* and **chi***p*).
Onset and Rime	• The first sound in a one-syllable word (e.g., *m* in *main*) is the onset. • The remainder of the one-syllable word (e.g., *ain* in *main*) is the rime.

OVERVIEW OF THE PRONUNCIATION LESSONS

The pronunciation lessons use **consonant pairs.**

Children who experience great difficulty in their ability to produce or hear letter sounds will benefit from the multisensory modeling of the letters that can be confused.

This practice can be run concurrently with the last three activities, at your discretion.

The forming of sound **consonant pairs** is given as follows:

Materials: Mirror

Methods: 1. *p, b*
"*Put your lips together, don't let any air out yet. Now suddenly make the sound like a popping sound and let the air out. Do it with me. Feel the air on your hands.*"

2. *t, d*
"*Feel your tongue on the back of your two front teeth; feel the top of your tongue as you say* **t.** *Do the same for* **d.**"

3. *k, g*
"*We are going to make a scraping sound in the back of our mouth. Watch what I do. Do it with me. What is happening to your tongue?*"

4. *f, v*
"*Rest your top teeth on your bottom lip and blow. Put your hand in front of your mouth and feel it. What do you feel?*"

5. *th, th* (soft and hard)
"*Let the tip of your tongue touch your top teeth. Watch as I do it. Do it with me. Put your hand in front of your mouth and listen to the sound.*"

6. *s, z*
"*Let's make a snake sound. Watch as I do it. Now let's do it together. Listen to the sound. Let's make a singing sound. Watch as I do it. Now let's do it together. Listen to the sound.*"

7. *ch, j*
"*Let's make a chopping sound. Listen and watch while I do it. Feel your jaw while we do it together. Let's make a jumping sound. It's from deeper in your throat. Listen and watch while I do it. Feel your throat while we do it together.*"

8. *sh, zh*
"*Put your finger in front of your lips and do what I do. Watch as I do it. Now let's do it together. Listen to the sound.*"

For additional practice, use the word list on the next page.

p	1.	pen play plain	nap cap ship	sap pup cup	help	
b	2.	boat bat baby	banana bank bench	crab grab club	rub	
t	3.	top tennis	tape tot	tip television	bit cat	sat chat
d	4.	dad dog food	dinner day	daffodil duck	bad sad	wood good
k	5.	king kiss	kind kit	key tick	tack took	clock ask
g	6.	good game	give gate	get gag	flag tag	lag wag
f	7.	fit full	frog friend	fancy staff	whiff cliff	beef chief
v	8.	van voice	violin visitor	vet live	give save	wave behave
th	9.	thin thank three	thought third thimble	thistle that	those south	mouth think
th	10.	with the	their them	then they	this	
s	11.	sat sing	so soap	sausage tops	glass kiss	floss cross
z	12.	zoo zebra	zap zipper	zone fizz	whiz quiz	jazz crazy
sh	13.	ship shall	shell she	sheep push	crush woosh	shoe leash
ch	14.	chin chip	chair china	chili chew	church such	much witch
j	15.	Jill Jack	just jump	jelly jet		

These are the **consonant pairs** to be dealt with
in the Pronunciation Section.

p	b
t	d
k	g
f	v
th (soft)	th (hard)
s	z
ch	j
sh	zh

AWARENESS OF WHOLE WORDS AS UNITS OF SOUND

✏ Activity 1

Aim: To give children an understanding that single words are separate units of sound

Learning Outcome:

> Children will respond accurately to single words, two-word strings, and three-word strings by moving cubes or counters into one, two, or three boxes.

Materials: Counters (three per child) or cubes
Fig. 1—A three-square grid per child
Fig. 2—Word list

Method:
1. Give out counters and grids. Explain that the children move a counter into a square (left-hand side preferred) if they hear one word only. Try this using the word "*Now.*" Check that all the group understood and responded correctly. Go on to try two words. The children should move two counters when you say the words "*Well done.*"

2. Say each item once only, as a rule. Repeat if someone is obviously lost. Let the children practice five single words followed by five two-word strings, as in the top section of Fig. 2.

(Continues on next page)

3. Demonstrate a three-word string such as "*We are here*." When everyone can do this, give the list of random one-, two-, and three-word strings, as in the bottom section of Fig. 2. The children move counters into the grid accordingly. If anyone hesitates, repeat the item as necessary to allow this child to succeed, but note on the record form that this was difficult for him or her.

Word List for Activity 1 (Fig. 2)

Run	Help me	Who can tell
Stop	Come here	Go to sleep
Talk	Sit down	Shut the door
Sleep	Run fast	Go to school
Jump	Jump high	Run the race

Random Word List for Activity 1

Swim	Play this game
Hop	Wait
What is that	Dive deep
Move fast	Tell your friend
Climb the tree	Jump high
Skip	Find your Dad
Dive	Look now

✎ Activity 2

Aim: To check that the concept of beginning, middle, end or first, second, last is clear

Learning Outcome:

Children will name pictures using the correct positional words of either *beginning, middle, end* or *first, second, last*.

Materials: Fig. 3—Animals
Fig. 4—Vehicles
Fig. 5—Children

Method:

1. Explain that when the children were listening to words and moving counters, they were also hearing a word that came first, a word that came second, and a word that came last. Or, as we sometimes say, beginning word, middle word, ending word, as in "Find your coat."

2. Show Fig. 3. Say, "*The lion is first (at the beginning); the giraffe is second (in the middle); the dog is last (at the end).*" Ask the children to name the position in line by pointing to the animals randomly and going around the group in turn.

3. Repeat with Fig. 4 (each vehicle has a well-known name).

4. Repeat with Fig. 5. This time say the names and have the children try to and say them also (e.g., "*Freda is first, Sam is second, and Tammy is third.*")

✎ Activity 3

Aim: To reinforce the concept of beginning, middle, end (and the alternative words of first, second, last)

Learning Outcome:

Children will name pictured children using *beginning, middle, end* correctly.

Materials: Figs. 6 and 7—Pictures of children in a row

Method:
1. Show Fig. 6. Remind the children about the words *first, second, last*.

2. Show Fig. 6 and introduce *beginning, middle, end*.

3. Show Fig. 7. Go around the group, asking the children to give the position words for Ben (at the beginning), Mary (in the middle), and Erin (at the end). Randomly ask, *"Where is Ben/Mary/Erin?"*

4. Now choose three children from the group to stand in a row and say, "I'm at the beginning/middle/end."

5. Ask the other children in the group to answer the question, *"Where is (name)?"* so that the answers are "At the beginning, in the middle, at the end."

6. Change the children around. Give everyone a turn.

Activity 4

Aim: To let the children understand that single words with two syllables are also whole words, and to practice responding to two-syllable and single words

Learning Outcome:

> Children will move counters or cubes into a grid in response to one, two, or three-word strings where the words may have two syllables.

Materials: Counters or cubes
Fig. 1—Grids, one copy per child
Fig. 8—Word list

Method:
1. Give out counters and grids as before.

2. Ask the children to move one or two counters into the grid in response to the word strings from Fig. 8.

Word List for Activity 4 (Fig. 8)

Jumped	Talked in class
Sleeping	Climbed up
Swimming	Sliding down
Hopped	Stopped
Skipped	The lion roared
Running	Helping me
Jumped high	Come outside
Shutting the door	Sitting down
Talked	Running fast
Slept until late	Waited there

(Continues on next page)

Who can tell

Diving deep

Diving

Looked out

Walked to school

Waited

The player ran

The clown juggled

The teacher spoke

Figure 1

Figure 2

Word List for Activity 1

Run	Help me	Who can tell
Stop	Come here	Go to sleep
Talk	Sit down	Shut the door
Sleep	Run fast	Go to school
Jump	Jump high	Run the race

Random Word List for Activity 1

Swim	Play this game
Hop	Wait
What is that	Dive deep
Move fast	Tell your friend
Climb the tree	Jump high
Skip	Find your Dad
Dive	Look now

Figure 3

Figure 4

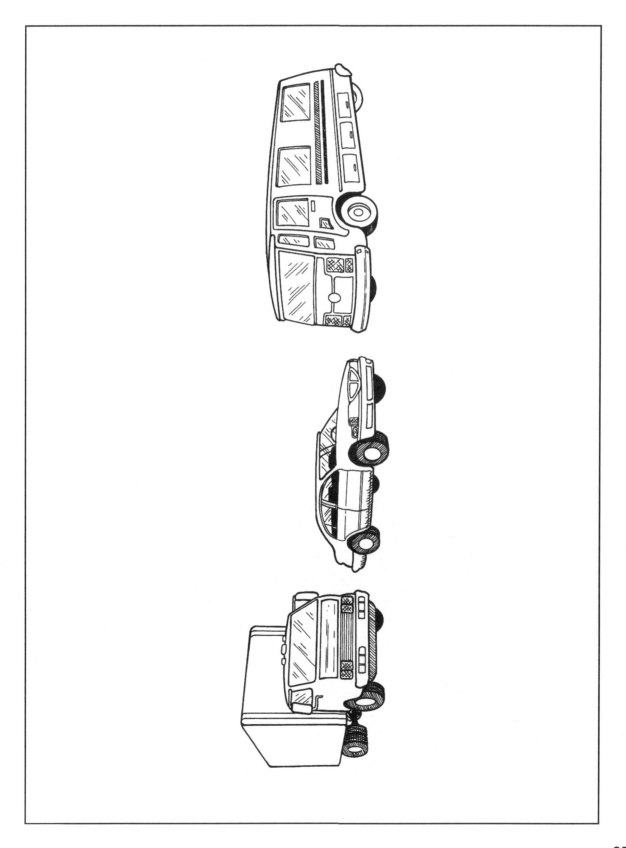

Figure 5

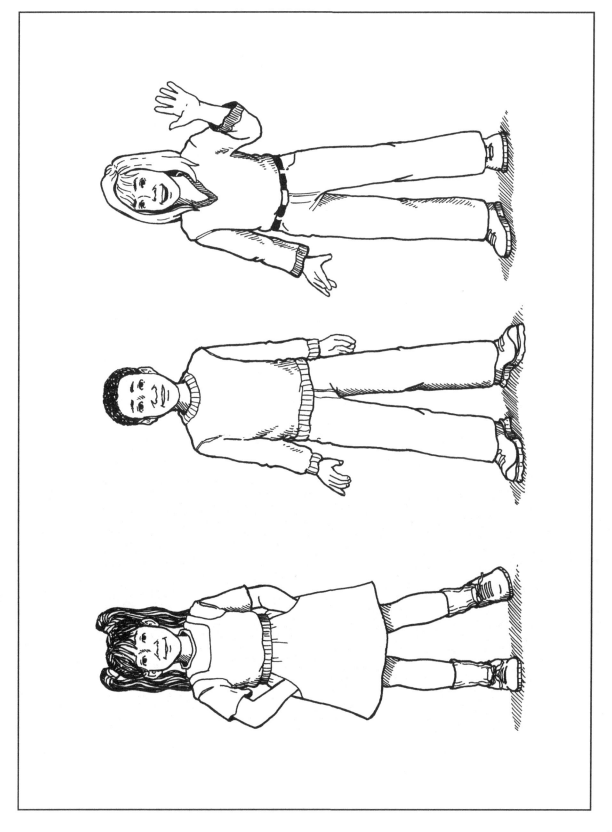

Figure 6

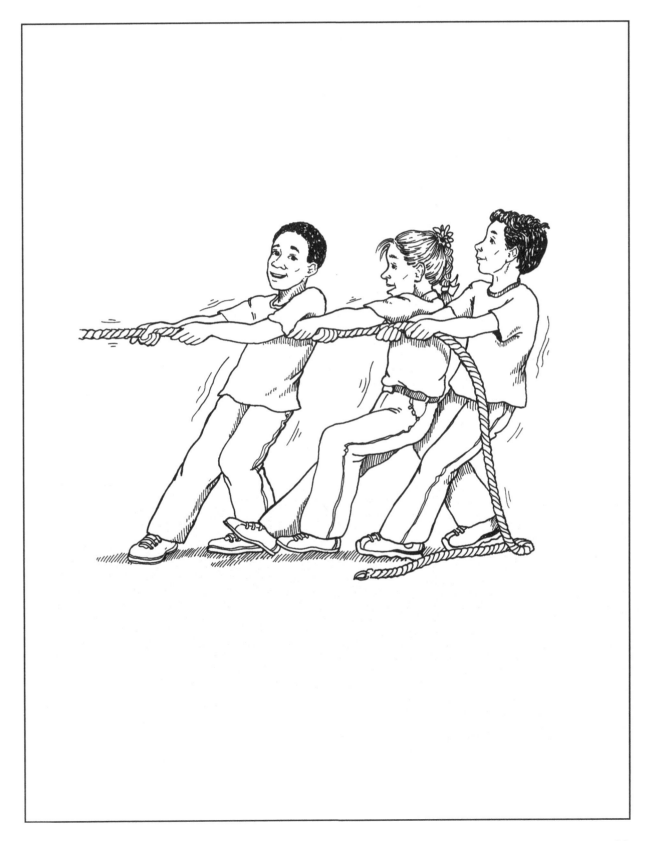

Figure 7

Figure 8

Word List for Activity 4

Jumped	Helping me
Sleeping	Come outside
Swimming	Sitting down
Hopped	Running fast
Skipped	Waited there
Running	Who can tell
Jumped high	Diving deep
Shutting the door	Diving
Talked	Looked out
Slept until late	Walked to school
Talked in class	Waited
Climbed up	The player ran
Sliding down	The clown juggled
Stopped	The teacher spoke
The lion roared	

TAPPING

Activity 1

Aim: To introduce a basic awareness of beats of sound

Learning Outcome:

> Children will produce their own beats of sound with an even rhythm up to three beats. Children will be able to repeat and invent loud/soft patterns.

Materials: A stick, drumstick, or small mallet per child
A paper plate (or similar object) to tap the beats per child

Method:

1. Ask the children to tap out one
one two
one two three,
even beats with about ½ second between each beat.

2. Ask the group to make one, two, or three beats at random.

3. Ask individuals to make one, two, or three beats at random.

4. Demonstrate a pattern of loud and soft beats. For example, / 0 /, where / = loud and 0 = soft.

5. Let the children practice a few patterns together, for example:
/ 0 0 / /
/ / 0 / / 0 / / 0 / /

6. Let children invent their own loud and soft patterns for the rest of the group to follow.

✎ Activity 2

Aim: To introduce a basic awareness of beats of sound

Learning Outcome: Children will produce their own beats of sound with an even rhythm up to three beats. Children will be able to repeat and invent loud/soft patterns.

Materials: A stick, drumstick, or small mallet per child
A paper plate (or similar object) to tap the beats per child

Method:
1. Follow the method for Activity 1 to give more children more practice.

2. Note any child who is having difficulty with this activity. Allow these children to have extra practice, with lots of encouragement.

✎ Activity 3

Aim: To link the understanding of beats with one-syllable words said as beats

Learning Outcome:

> Children will respond to names with one, two, or three syllables by tapping the equivalent number of times.

Materials: A stick, drumstick, or small mallet per child
A paper plate (or similar object) per child
Fig. 9—Word list of names

Method:

1. Remind the children that single words can have two beats in them, as they found out when they were moving counters. This time they are going to pick out the beats in words.

2. Let each child in the group say his or her own name while the others tap the correct number of beats right after listening.

3. Use the list of names in Fig. 9 to give further practice. Let the children respond as a group and point to individuals at random.

4. Use some other words with varied number of syllables to get tapping patterns.

5. Watch for any children having difficulty with this activity. Note on their record forms to ask for extra help at home. Give these children very positive feedback at the level where they do succeed (e.g., one beat).

(Continues on next page)

Word List for Activity 3 (Fig. 9)

Susan	Tom
Henry	Louise
Alison	Carlos
Christine	Rebecca
Mark	Armand
David	Vanessa
Benjamin	Matthew
Stephen	John
Ann	Juliet
Maria	June

✎ Activity 4

Aim: To give further practice at tapping one to four beats for syllables in words

Learning Outcome:

> Children will respond to category words with one, two, three, or four syllables by tapping the equivalent number of times.

Materials: Drumsticks and plates as used in Activity 3
Fig. 10—Word list

Method:

1. Give the first 10 words in Fig. 10 for the children to practice with the drumsticks and plates as in Activity 3. Or use the children's own names again.

2. Use the remainder of the words in Fig. 10 to have the children respond in the following way: tap upper arm (**first** syllable), lower arm (**second** syllable), left knee (**third** syllable), right knee (**fourth** syllable).

3. Again, look for any children not doing this activity easily and decide where they find difficulty—1, 2, 3, or 4 syllables.

4. You may wish to provide copies of the word list for extra practice at home.

(Continues on next page)

Word List for Activity 4 (Fig. 10)

cup	gate	car	cat
soup	path	train	dog
plate	garden	airplane	headache
teapot	flower pot	motorbike	pig
knife	daisy	van	lion
fork	rose	helicopter	tiger
spoon	dandelion	rocket	crocodile
tablecloth	tulip	boat	giraffe
frying pan	carnation	bicycle	zebra
saucer	daffodil	wagon	elephant

Figure 9

Word List for Activity 3

Susan	Tom
Henry	Louise
Alison	Carlos
Christine	Rebecca
Mark	Armand
David	Vanessa
Benjamin	Matthew
Stephen	John
Ann	Juliet
Maria	June

Figure 10

Word List for Activity 4

cup	gate	car	cat
soup	path	train	dog
plate	garden	airplane	headache
teapot	flower pot	motorbike	pig
knife	daisy	van	lion
fork	rose	helicopter	tiger
spoon	dandelion	rocket	crocodile
tablecloth	tulip	boat	giraffe
frying pan	carnation	bicycle	zebra
saucer	daffodil	wagon	elephant

Word List for Activity

soup	bath	spab	
tea	quilt		
		tiger	
spoon	dandelion	coaster	crocus
tablecloth	tulip	boat	giraffe
frying pan	carnation	bicycle	zebra
saucer	daffodil	wagon	elephant

RHYME

✎ Activity 1

Aim: To introduce the concept of rhyme at an enjoyment level

Learning Outcome:

> Children will repeat nonsense rhymes as members of a group.

Materials: Nonsense rhymes outlined below

Method:

1. Use the following nonsense rhymes to have fun as you supply the word that rhymes. The children can join in as a group if they can guess the missing word.

2. Follow this by having everyone say the nonsense rhymes one or more times together as a group.

   On a bicycle comes a long thin **snake**.
   Will he stop?
   No, he can't find the _____ (brake).

   I can hear something that goes tick **tock**.
   It tells us the time
   And it's called a _____ (clock).

   A long time ago there lived a **king**
   Who got a sore throat
   And couldn't _____ (sing).

   When at last the king got **well**,
   He didn't sing,
   He rang a _____ (bell).

(Continues on next page)

In the middle of the night in my **house**
Something squeaks.
I'm sure it's a _____ (mouse).

Guess what food is in my **dish**?
Is it meat
Or is it _____ (fish)?

✎ Activity 2

Aim: To let the children know whether pairs of words, given verbally, rhyme or not

Learning Outcome:

> Children will respond verbally to whether two words rhyme or not.

Materials: Fig. 11—Word list

Method:

1. Explain that you are going to say a pair of words like *mouse* and *house*. Ask the children to say "yes" if the words rhyme and "no" if they don't.

2. Give more practice with *dog* and *cat*. Go through the word list and let the children answer as a group.

3. Notice if any particular child is unable to tell whether the words rhyme or not, and support that child quickly.

4. Continue with group responses.

(Continues on next page)

Word List for Activity 2 (Fig. 11)

night, light

day, say

far, car

far, wide

mitt, sit

rain, pain

rain, snow

snow, go

dark, light

light, white

red, bed

chair, hair

cake, lake

read, feed

bird, word

knee, tree

🖉 Activity 3

Aim: To give further practice in the identification of rhyming pairs by using picture stimulus sheets on which the children can make their responses

Learning Outcome:

> Children will respond by coloring in the figure when they find and say a rhyming pair of words.

Materials: Figs. 12 and 13—Picture stimulus sheets, one copy of each per child; Pencils or crayons

Method:
1. Give each child a copy of Fig. 12.

2. Go around the group, asking children in turn to name the pairs of pictures.

3. Go around the group, asking children to say the words for each pair of pictures and also to say "yes" if the words rhyme and "no" if they don't.

4. Model for the children how to color in the rhyming pairs and to leave blank those that do not rhyme.

5. Let the children do this for both picture sheets (Figs. 12 and 13). They can have support from one another.

Picture Words on Fig. 12

mouse, house

man, fan

frog, log

dog, cat

rake, snake

Picture Words on Fig. 13

ring, moon

sock, clock

king, ring

bed, spoon

sun, moon

✏ Activity 4

Aim: To give further practice in the identification of rhyming pairs by using picture stimulus sheets on which the children can make their responses

Learning Outcome:

Children will respond by coloring in the figure when they find and say a rhyming pair of words.

Materials: Figs. 14 and 15—Picture stimulus sheets, one copy of each per child; Pencils or crayons

Method:
1. Give each child a copy of Fig. 14.

2. Go around the group, asking children in turn to name the pairs of pictures.

3. Go around the group, asking children to say the words for each pair of pictures and also to say "yes" if the words rhyme and "no" if they don't.

4. Model for the children how to color in the rhyming pairs and to leave blank those that do not rhyme.

5. Let the children do this for both picture sheets (Figs. 14 and 15). They can have support from one another.

Picture Words on Fig. 14   Picture Words on Fig. 15

Picture Words on Fig. 14	Picture Words on Fig. 15
box, fox	star, car
shoe, sock	star, sun
bee, key	hat, cat
chair, pear	three, tree
boat, coat	hat, fan

✏ Activity 5

Aim: To give further practice with rhyming pairs

Learning Outcome:

> Children will supply a picture of a word whose name rhymes with a stimulus picture word.

Materials: Figs. 12, 13, 14, and 15—Pictures, one copy of each figure cut up into individual pictures for the adult; one sheet cut up for each child (It does not matter if two children have the same set of pictures.)

Plastic storage bags to separate picture sets

Method:

1. Place one picture in the center of the group (table top or floor) and ask, "*Who can put a picture that rhymes next to this picture?*" More than one child might be able to do this.

2. When each child has had at least two turns, place together two pictures that do **not** rhyme. Ask for a picture that rhymes with either one of these two pictures.

3. Emphasize to the children that, for example, *fish* and *dish* rhyme with each other, but not with *sock*. *Sock* is the odd one out.

4. Play the "odd one out" version of the game several times.

✎ Activity 6

Aim: To give practice at selecting rhyming pairs from three word pictures

Learning Outcome: Children will pick out, say, and color two words that rhyme from a group of three pictures.

Materials: Figs. 16 and 17—Picture sheets, one copy of each per child
Pencils or crayons

Method: 1. Demonstrate to the children how to say the names of the pictures first. Then ask the question, "*Which two words rhyme?*"

2. Model how to color the two in each row that rhyme and to leave blank the odd one out.

3. Ask the children to complete their sheets.

Picture Words on Fig. 16

hen, pen, book

cat, dog, hat

fan, man, log

pig, pen, wig

sock, frog, log

Picture Words on Fig. 17

snail, nail, bag

sail, mat, tail

key, clock, lock

ring, king, queen

sock, snake, lock

🖉 Activity 7

Aim: To practice finding the odd one out from three-word strings (including a rhyming pair) given orally

Learning Outcome:

> Children will say the odd word out with picture support and then without picture support.

Materials: Fig. 18—Picture sheets, one copy per child
Pencils

Figs. 16 and 17, Picture sheets

Method: 1. Give each child a copy of Fig. 18 to review Activity 6.

Picture Words on Fig. 18
block, lock, train
fish, pear, bear
fox, jug, , box
two, house, shoe
cake, fish, dish

2. As a group, say each of the picture words in each line. Ask, "*Which is the odd one out?*" Let the children answer as a group.

3. Ask the children to work on their picture sheets, but this time to put a cross on the odd one out in each line.

4. Now name each picture in Figs. 16 and 17 to give practice at finding the odd one out in three-word items given orally.

✎ Activity 8

Aim:	To give experience of supplying a rhyming word (using pictures)

Learning Outcome:

> Children will see, say, and select a third rhyming word to put with two other rhyming words.

Materials: Figs. 19, 20, 21, and 22—Picture sheets, one copy of each per child
Scissors
Glue or glue sticks

Method:

1. Hand out a copy of Fig. 19 to each child.

2. Hand out copies of Fig. 20 and model cutting up the pictures.

3. Ask the children to name each picture in a pair on Fig. 19, and then to look for the third rhyming word in their separate pictures. Show them how to glue the rhyming word in place and repeat all three words that rhyme.

4. If there is time, do the same activity with Figs. 21 and 22 (or save this for an additional activity).

Picture Words on Fig. 19

snail, nail
frog, log
fan, man
clock, lock
cake, snake

Picture Words on Fig. 20

sock
pan
tail
rake
dog

(Continues on next page)

Picture Words on Fig. 21

ring, king

three, tree

car, jar

bear, pear

bat, cat

Picture Words on Fig. 22

square

guitar

hat

key

wing

Figure 11

Word List for Activity 2

night, light

day, say

far, car

far, wide

mitt, sit

rain, pain

rain, snow

snow, go

dark, light

light, white

red, bed

chair, hair,

cake, lake

read, feed

bird, word

knee, tree

Figure 12

Figure 13

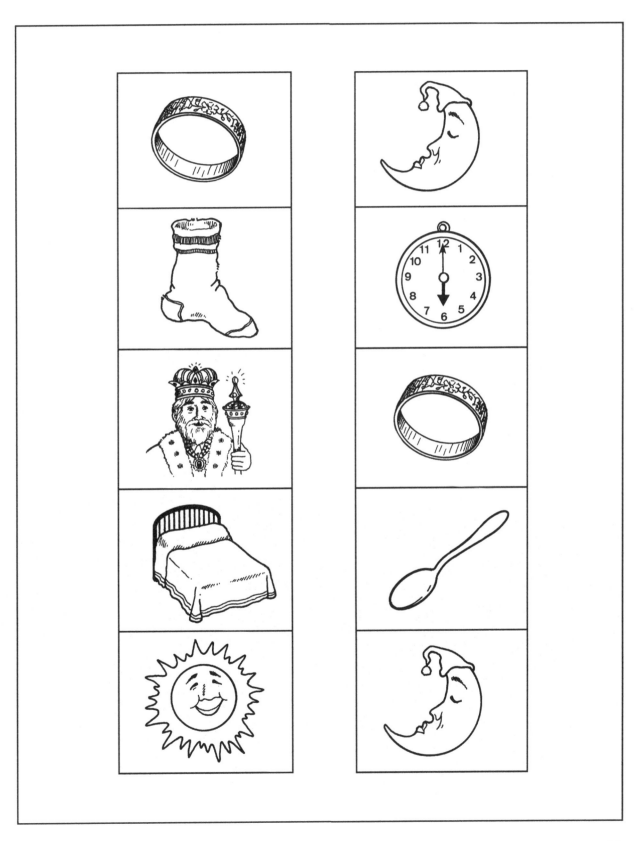

Figure 14

Figure 15

Figure 16

Figure 17

Figure 18

Rhyme

Figure 19

Figure 20

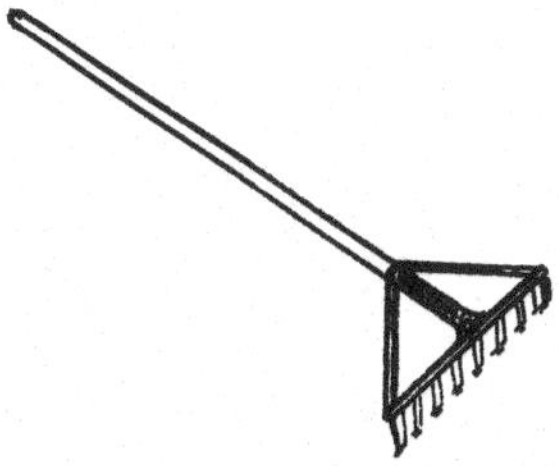

Figure 21

Figure 22

		☐

ONSET AND RIME

✏ Activity 1

Aim: To introduce the concept of splitting onsets and rimes in a striking way

Learning Outcome: Children will respond verbally to produce both onset and rimes.

Materials: Two toy cars
Two marbles
Ruler
Containers, one very small and one larger

Method:

1. Ask children to "*Listen and look.*"
Say, "*Watch these two cars.*" Make cars collide. "*What has happened?*" Encourage different ways of saying the answer.

2. Roll a marble down the tilted ruler into a container small enough to hold that marble and one other without the marbles rolling around. Say, "*What has happened?*" Again encourage different ways of describing the collision.

3. Divide the children into two groups. Use the following words so that the children can say either onset or rime while the cars collide or marbles roll. For example, with the word *cat*, Group One says "/c/" while one car moves toward the other car. Group Two says "/at/" loudly when the cars collide.

(Continues on next page)

Make several games of this using cars and marbles.
The groups can stand up and move, holding the cars
and making the onset/rime sounds.

Suitable words for these games are:

cat	mat
jet	red
big	win
dog	pop
jump	run

✎ Activity 2

Aim: To have children identify a word when spoken in onset and rime format

Learning Outcome:

Children will use their understanding of the concept of onset and rime to respond.

Materials: Fig. 23—Word List 1 (first column)
Fig. 24—Pictures of Word List 1
Hand puppet

Method:

1. Say, "*Let's name these pictures. This is Percy the Puppet who has a funny voice. He says words in a bumpy way. Listen to see if you can tell which word he is saying.*"

2. Show the first two pictures. Have the puppet say, "*/c/—/at/.*" Ask, "*What did he say?*"

3. Point to the cat. "*Look at the two pictures. Listen to Percy the Puppet. What did he say?*"

4. Practice using all the pictures in Fig. 24 with the group.

5. Ensure each child has a turn.

(*Continues on next page*)

Word List 1 (Fig. 23)

cat	bat
leg	pen
pig	lip
dog	pot
cup	bud
mat	rat
bed	hen
wig	tin
log	doll
sun	run

Picture Words on Fig. 24

cat	mat
leg	bed
pig	wig
dog	log
cup	sun

✏ Activity 3

Aim: To have children identify a word when spoken in onset and rime format

Learning Outcome:
> Children will use their understanding of the concept of onset and rime to respond.

Materials:
Fig. 23—Word List 1 (second column)
Fig. 25—Pictures of Word List 1
Hand puppet
Crayons, red and blue for each child

Method:
1. Point to the pictures at the top of Fig. 25.

2. Say, "*Let's name these pictures. This is Percy the Puppet who has a funny voice. He says words in a bumpy way. Listen to see if you can tell which word he is saying.*"

3. Show the first two pictures. Have the puppet say, "/b/—/at/." Ask, "*What did he say?*"

4. Point to the next pictures. "*Listen to Percy the Puppet. What did he say?*"

5. Practice using all the pictures in this set with the group.

6. Ensure that each child has a turn.

Picture Words on Fig. 25

bat	rat
pen	hen
lip	tin
pot	doll
bud	run

✏ Activity 4

Aim: To extend an understanding of onset/rime from pictures to words using manipulatives

Learning Outcome:

> Children will be able to build with blocks to show how a word can be divided into onset and rime.

Materials: Three blocks or three colored cubes
Fig. 23—Word List 1

Method:

1. Show 3 blocks and say, "*We have been splitting words like this—one block for the beginning and two for the end. When the puppet says /c/—/at/, the blocks are like this. What word is that?*" Children will answer, "cat." "*Let's move our blocks together and all say* cat."

2. Using the word list, do several words together as a group. Next, ensure that each child has a turn.

3. Practice using three stackable cubes split into one and two joined together, as an extension of the activity.

✎ Activity 5

Aim: To extend an understanding of onset/rime from pictures to words using manipulatives

Learning Outcome:

> Children will be able to build with blocks to show how a word can be divided into onset and rime.

Materials: Fig. 26—Grid (Move it and Say it)
Three colored cubes per child
Fig. 27—Word List 2

Method:

1. Show three colored cubes and say, "*We have been splitting words like this—one block for the beginning and two for the end. Now we'll use these cubes.*" Give out the colored cubes. "*When the puppet says /r/—/at/, the cubes are like this. What word is that?*" Children answer "*rat.*" "*Let's move our cubes together and all say rat.*"

2. Give each child a copy of Fig. 26. "*Let's practice moving the cubes as we say the words.*" Say, "*/j/—/et/. Let's move our cubes.*" Move the cubes and say "*jet*" while the children watch and practice.

3. Using the words in Fig. 27, do several words together as a group. Next, ensure that each child has a turn.

(*Continues on next page*)

Word List 2 (Fig. 27)

rat	hat
jet	pet
bit	sit
lot	not
fun	bun
sat	ram
red	bet
fit	win
got	rod
put	pull

Figure 23

Word List 1

cat	bat
leg	pen
pig	lip
dog	pot
cup	bud
mat	rat
bed	hen
wig	tin
log	doll
sun	run

Figure 24

Figure 25

Figure 26

Figure 27

Word List 2

rat	hat
jet	pet
bit	sit
lot	not
fun	bun
sat	ram
red	bet
fit	win
got	rod
put	pull

SEGMENTATION OF WORDS INTO SYLLABLES

✏ Activity 1

Aim: To teach children to break words into parts (i.e., two to four syllables)

Learning Outcome:

> Children will split names into parts using colored cubes.

Materials: Pencils, crayons, pictures and/or interlocking building toys
Four colored cubes per student
Fig. 28—List of children's names

Method:

1. Demonstrate ways of breaking up whole things (e.g., pencil, crayon, pictures, and/or building toys). This is meant to be a dramatic way of showing splitting (not to be copied by student). Give each child four cubes attached together (any colors).

2. Ask the children to listen to the name "*Susan*" and split their cubes into two parts to show the two parts of the word. Do this splitting with them and check that each child has done it correctly.

3. Practice splitting the names of the children in the group using the cubes. Give more practice from the list of names (Fig. 28).

4. Ask the children to blend the syllables or word parts together and say the whole word after each word is segmented.

(Continues on next page)

Name List for Activity 1 (Fig. 28)

Susan	Tom
Henry	Louise
Alison	Carlos
Christine	Rebecca
Mark	Armand
David	Vanessa
Benjamin	Matthew
Stephen	John
Ann	Juliet
Maria	Jane

Activity 2

Aim: To teach children to break words into two to four syllables

Learning Outcome:
Children will respond to the number of syllables in a word by showing the correct number of fingers or clapping the correct number of times.

Materials: Colored cubes
Fig. 29—Word list

Method:
1. Use colored cubes to show the parts of words from Fig. 29 to review two- to four-syllable words.

2. Ask children to show the syllables by using their fingers or by clapping. Get them to respond to the words in Fig. 29 in this order: together, individually around the group, and with closed eyes. Model each new way of responding.

3. Ask children to blend the syllables or word parts together and say the whole word after each word is segmented.

(*Continues on next page*)

Word List for Activity 2 (Fig. 29)

Two Syllable	Three Syllable	Four Syllable
pillow	telephone	caterpillar
yellow	dinosaur	helicopter
purple	basketball	television
balloon	hamburger	alligator
hello	crocodile	kindergarten
baseball	bicycle	macaroni
skateboard	tricycle	supermarket
playground	astronaut	watermelon
picnic	cucumber	
puppy	lemonade	
pizza	yesterday	
birthday	beautiful	
sunset	difficult	
rainbow	photograph	
	hospital	
	animal	
	together	
	spaghetti	
	computer	
	buttercup	
	strawberry	

Activity 3

Aim: To help children break words into two to four syllables

Learning Outcome:

Children will move cubes into boxes on a grid to correspond to the number of syllables in a word as they say the word.

Materials: Fig. 29—Word list for Activity 2
Four colored cubes or sticks per child
Fig. 30—Laminated grid with four boxes, one per child

Method:

1. Review previous learning by reminding the children how to split a two-syllable, a three-syllable, and a four-syllable word into parts with the sticks or colored cubes.

2. Hand out copies of Fig. 30 and cubes. Say, "*Watch where I keep my cubes. I put them in the shopping cart. Now I will say the word and move my cube for each separate part of the word: Su—san. Now let's all do this together using another word: breakfast. Let's try it again for a longer word: boomerang.*"

3. "*Now I will say a word and you will move your cubes for the parts of the word you hear. Remember to say the word as you move the cubes.*"

4. Ask the children to blend the syllables or word parts together and say the whole word after each word is segmented.

✎ Activity 4

Aim: To help children blend words into two to four syllables

Learning Outcome:

Children will identify and blend word parts into whole words.

Materials: Hand puppet
Fig. 29—Word list of mixed two-, three-, four-syllable words

Method:

1. Tell the children to listen carefully to the puppet because he speaks in a funny voice. Make the puppet say the words in Fig. 29, broken into syllables. Have the children say the whole word. As usual, model the expected response first.

2. Now let individual children, in turn, say their responses to the puppet.

3. Now let the children in turn have the puppet and whisper a word that they can make the puppet say. The group responds with the whole word.

4. Ask the children to blend the syllables or word parts together and say the whole word after each word is segmented.

✎ Activity 5

Aim: To consolidate the understanding of syllable splitting by supplying ending syllables

Learning Outcome:

> Children will supply the final syllable of a two-syllable word after hearing the first part.

Materials: Word list of things in the classroom

Method:
1. Say, *"Let's find some words for things in the classroom that have two parts. Let's play a game with these words. The game is called What's Left? I can see, for example, a window*
   pencil
   paper
   carpet
   blackboard

2. *"Now I will say the word _____ and you say it too. Now I am going to say the first part and you give me the part that's left."*

   pen—cil
   win—dow

3. Use your word list to go around the group, requesting the children to supply the end part of the words.

4. Ask the children to blend the syllables or word parts together and say the whole word after each word is segmented.

Figure 28

Name List for Activity 1

Susan	Tom
Henry	Louise
Alison	Carlos
Christine	Rebecca
Mark	Armand
David	Vanessa
Benjamin	Matthew
Stephen	John
Ann	Juliet
Maria	Jane

Figure 29

Word List for Activity 2

Two Syllable	Three Syllable	Four Syllable
pillow	telephone	caterpillar
yellow	dinosaur	helicopter
purple	basketball	television
balloon	hamburger	alligator
hello	crocodile	kindergarten
baseball	bicycle	macaroni
skateboard	tricycle	supermarket
playground	astronaut	watermelon
picnic	cucumber	
puppy	lemonade	
pizza	yesterday	
birthday	beautiful	
sunset	difficult	
rainbow	photograph	
	hospital	
	animal	
	together	
	spaghetti	
	computer	
	buttercup	
	strawberry	

One Syllable	Two Syllable	Three Syllable

Figure 30

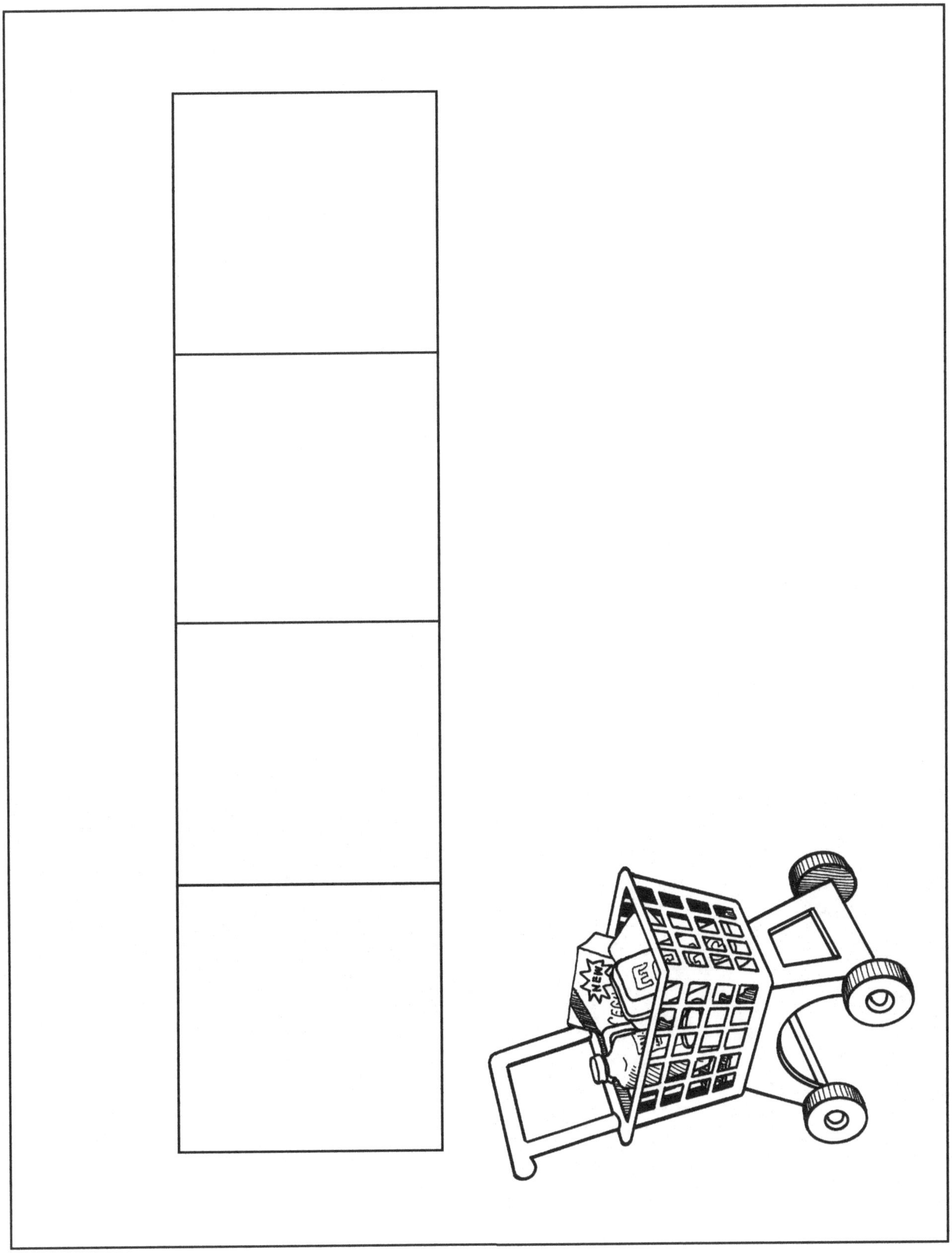

SEGMENTATION OF WORDS INTO PHONEMES

Activity 1

Aim: To introduce the concept of segmenting words into phonemes

Learning Outcome:

> Children will cut a picture of a word into the correct number of parts for the number of phonemes in the word, saying the phonemes separately as they do so.

Materials: Copies of Figs. 31–36
- Fig. 31—cow   Fig. 34—fish
- Fig. 32—arm   Fig. 35—bed
- Fig. 33—car   Fig. 36—cake

Scissors

Crayons

Method:

1. Give each child a picture showing two parts. Ask them to cut along the line.

2. Ask the children to put the pieces together and say the word as a whole, followed by the word split into its phonemes: c—ow
                                                    ar—m
                                                    c—ar

3. Give the children the pictures of words with three phonemes and follow the same steps. The phonemes are   f—i—sh
                                                    b—e—d
                                                    c—a—ke

(Continues on next page)

114 Launch Into Reading Success

4. Now let the children choose one of the pictures to color.

5. Use the time while the children color to give many auditory prompts about the phonemes in the words.

f—i—sh

6. Encourage the children to point and say the phoneme as they color the relevant part of the picture.

✎ Activity 2

Aim: To introduce the concept of segmenting words into phonemes in a different way

Learning Outcome:

> Children will move cubes and say the phoneme parts of word pictures.

Materials: Figs. 31–36—Pictures, laminated copy of each
Three colored cubes for each child

Method:

1. Name the pictures with the children. Choose one picture with only two phonemes (car, arm, or cow) and put it in the middle of the group.

2. Give each child two colored cubes. Ask someone to put one cube in each part of the picture and support him or her in saying the phonemes,

   e.g., c—ar, or
   c—ow, or
   ar—m.

3. Do the same with the other two-phoneme pictures and ensure children say the phonemes as the cubes are placed. Randomly ask the children to place the cubes and say the phonemes.

4. Repeat the process with the three-phoneme pictures.

Figure 31

Figure 32

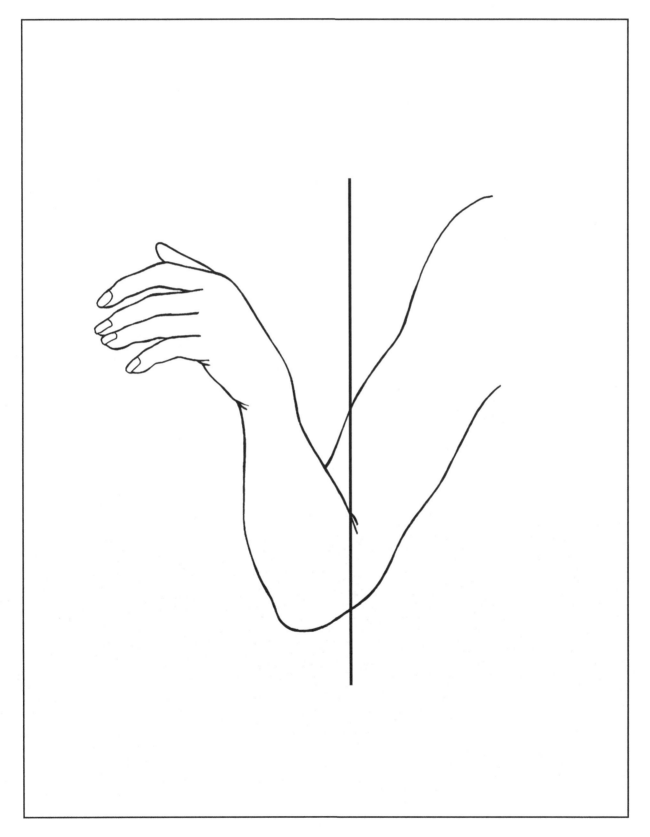

Figure 33

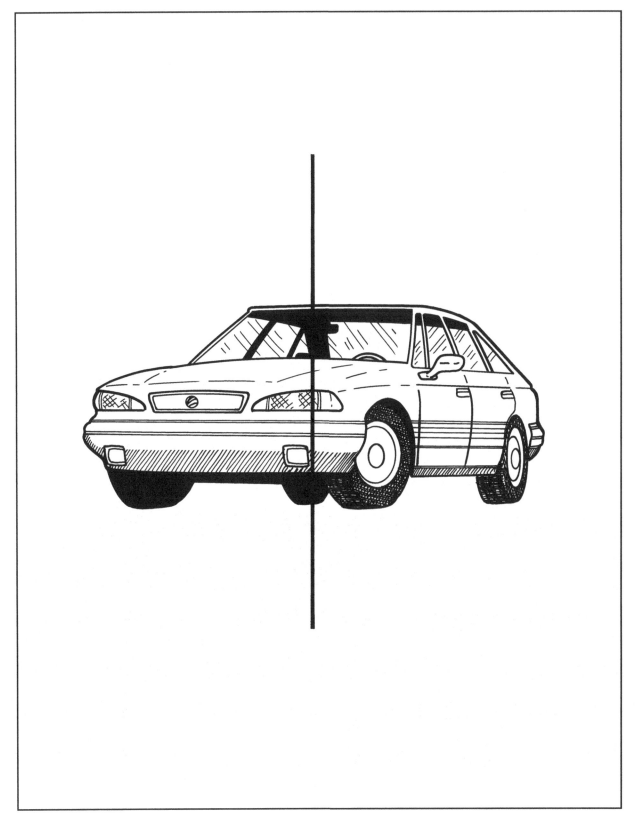

Figure 34

Figure 35

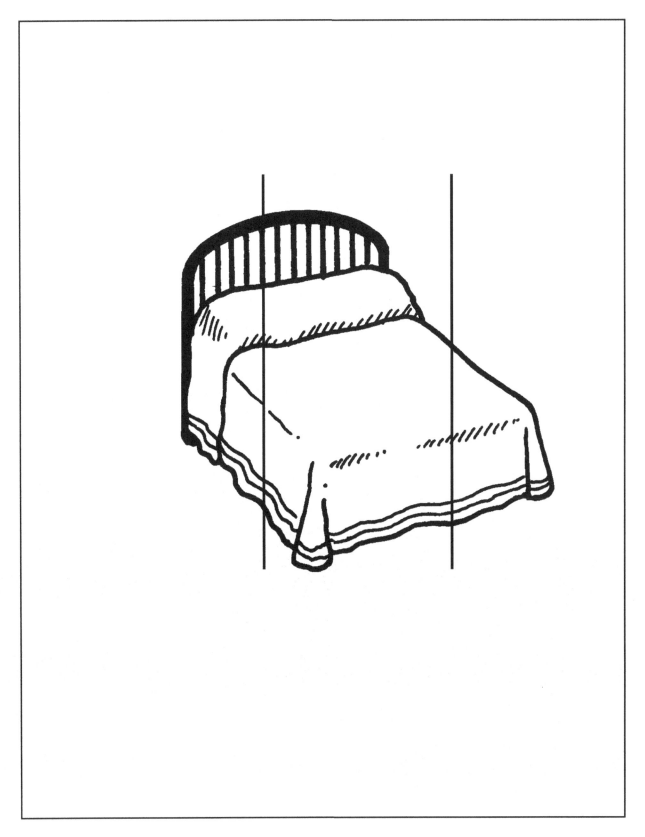

Figure 36

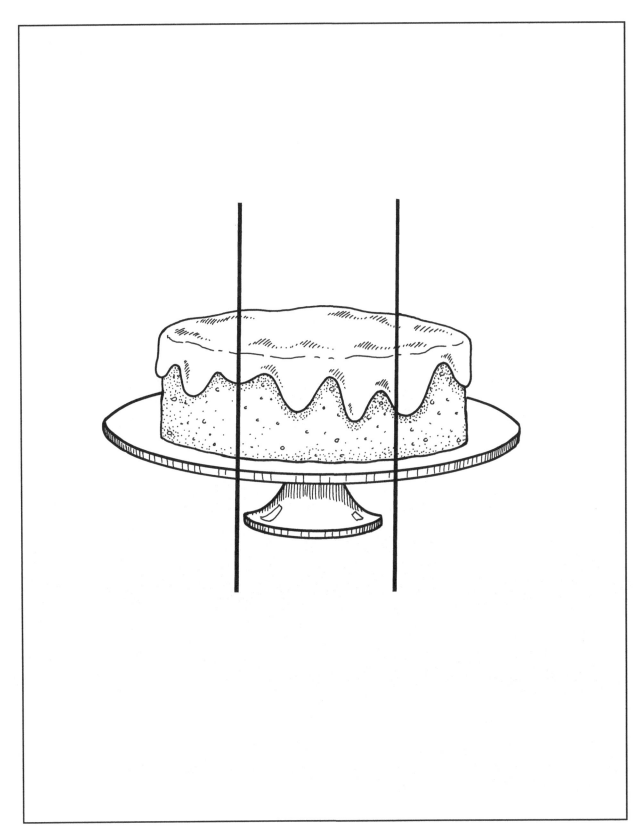

DISCRIMINATION

✎ Activity 1

Aim: To introduce children to the concept of beginning sounds in words

Learning Outcome:

> Children can name pictures that begin with the same sound.

Materials: Fig. 37—Word List 1
Fig. 38—Pictures
Fig. 39—Cut up individual pictures:
fish   man   sun   pen   ring
fan   mop   soap   pig   rope

Method:
1. Say, "*Let's name these pictures.*"
   Children and teacher name the pictures in Fig. 38.

2. Point to the picture of the ring. "*This is a rrrring.*"
   Ring begins with rrr. Let's say it together—
   */r/ **ring**. Listen to other words that begin like **ring**.*"
   Say the words in Fig. 37.

3. Put the individual pictures of the fish and fan on the table. Say, "***fish** and **fan** begin with the same sound.*"

4. Say the two words slowly. Children take turns to say the names of the two pictures that begin with the same sound.

5. Do the same with the other pairs of pictures.

(Continues on next page)

Match the separate pictures with those in Fig. 38.

6. Use Fig. 37 to give the children more practice (auditory only) at identifying words that begin with the same sound.

Word List 1 for Activity 1 (Fig. 37)

robin

rose

ride

rhyme

ravioli

rot

rat

rip

run

ribbon

✎ Activity 2

Aim: To have children respond verbally as to whether two picture words begin with the same sound

Learning Outcome:

Children will know the pictures that begin with the same sound.

Materials: Fig. 39—Cut up individual pictures
fish   man   sun   pen   ring
fan   mop   soap   pig   rope

Method:

1. Show two pictures. Children and teacher name the two pictures.

2. Ask, "*Do these picture words begin with the same sound? Let's say them together. Do the pictures begin with the same sound?*"

3. Practice with pairs of pictures until all the pictures are used.

4. If a response is incorrect, say to the child, "*No,(name). Listen.*" Say the name of the picture slowly. Child repeats name slowly.

5. Practice using pairs of pictures. These may be the separate pictures used in Activity 1, which can be put in different combinations.

✎ Activity 3

Aim: To have children respond verbally as to whether two of three picture words begin with the same sound

Learning Outcome:

> Children will discriminate which pictures begin with the same sound.

Materials: Fig. 39—One copy per child; one copy cut into individual pictures
Pictures from Fig. 39 to be cut up separately:
fish   man   sun   pen   ring
fan   mop   soap   pig   rope

Method:

1. Review the names of the pictures. Put three individual picture words on the table, two of which begin with the same sound and one other. Name the pictures. Ask, "*Which two pictures have the same beginning sound?*" Practice with all the pairs.

2. Give children two pairs of pictures. Ask children to put together the picture words that begin with the same sound.

3. If children respond incorrectly, say, "*No, (name) . Listen.*" Match the correct pair of pictures. Say the beginning sound slowly (e.g., "**fffffan, fffffish.** *Both start with* **fffffan, fffffish.** *The beginning sound is the same*").

4. Place all the pictures on the table. Play a game. Choose one picture and have the children show the other picture that begins with the same sound.

🖉 Activity 4

Aim: To let children respond verbally as to whether two words begin with the same sound, with and without picture prompts

Learning Outcome:

> Children can tell if two words begin with the same sound.

Materials: Fig. 39—Pictures
Fig. 40—Word List 2
Fig. 41—Game board
Markers for game board

Method:
1. Name the pictures in Fig. 39 and have the children join in.

2. Say the names of two pictures and ask the children, "*Do these two picture words begin the same?*" Children answer "Yes" or "No."

3. "*Let's practice with some more words. Just listen. There are no pictures. Do these two words begin the same?*" Say the words in Fig. 40. Children answer "Yes" or "No."

4. Make sure each child gets a turn.

5. Now introduce the game board (Fig. 41). Let individual children move a marker on the game board if they answer correctly to pairs of words from Fig. 40.

6. Randomly choose some pairs that begin the same and some that do not.

(*Continues on next page*)

Word List 2 for Activity 4 (Fig. 40)

ring	rhyme	fish	figure
road	rid	fan	funny
rock	ride	fun	fist
robin	rut	from	for
rose	ravioli	Frank	fig
man	Mike	sun	saddle
money	middle	soap	sorry
most	mouse	sad	sick
mud	mint	sack	sing
mist	motorcycle	soon	set
pen	pond		
pig	parrot		
penny	pencil		
picture	people		
pole	park		

✐ Activity 5

Aim: To let children positively identify whether two words begin with the same sound

Learning Outcome:

> Children will respond verbally and by coloring as to whether two words begin with the same sound.

Materials: Figs. 42, 43, and 44—Picture sheets, one copy of each per child
Crayons

Method:

1. Say two words. Ask the children, "*Do these two words begin the same?*"

2. Give out the picture sheets. Model how to color the pictures that begin with the same sound. Say, "*If they do not begin the same, leave the pictures blank.*"

3. Have the children complete their sheets.

✎ Activity 6

Aim: To introduce children to the concept of ending sounds in words

Learning Outcome:

Children will name the pictures that end with the same sound.

Materials: Fig. 45—Word List 3
Figs. 46 and 47—Picture sheets

Method:
1. Say, "*Let's name these pictures.*" Children and teacher name the pictures in Figs. 46 and Fig. 47.

2. Point to the cat. "*This is a **catttt.** Cat ends with **ttt.** Let's say it together—**cat.** Listen to other words that end like **cat.**" Say other words that end like *cat* (e.g., *mat, hat, bat, sat*).

3. Point to the first two pictures in Fig. 47. Say, "**cat** and **feet** *end with the same sound.*"

4. Say the words slowly. Children take turns to say the names of the two pictures that end with the same sound.

5. Do the same with the other pairs of pictures in Fig. 47.

6. Use Fig. 45 to give the children more practice (auditory only) at identifying words that end with the same sound.

Word List 3 for Activity 6 (Fig. 45)

street	put
seat	sat
meat	fat
cheat	bit
heat	pit

✐ Activity 7

Aim: To let children respond verbally as to whether the names of the two pictures end with the same sound

Learning Outcome:

Children will name the pictures that end with the same sound.

Materials: Fig. 47—Picture sheet, two copies (one cut up and one left whole)

Method:

1. Show two pictures on the whole Fig. 47. Children and teacher name the two pictures.

2. Ask, "*Do these pictures end with the same sound? Let's say them together. Do the pictures end with the same sound?*"

3. Now mix up the cut-up pictures.

4. Practice by showing two pictures at a time, asking the children if the words sound the same at the end.

5. If a response is incorrect, say to the child, "*No, (name). Listen.*" Say the name of the picture. Child repeats name.

Activity 8

Aim: To let children positively identify whether two words end with the same sound

Learning Outcome:

Children will respond verbally and by coloring as to whether two words end with the same sound.

Materials: Figs. 48, 49, and 50—Picture sheets, one copy of each per child
Crayons

Method:
1. Say two words. Ask the children, "*Do these two words end with the same sound?*"

2. Hand out picture sheets. Model how to color pictures that end with the same sound. Say, "*If they do not end the same, leave the pictures blank.*"

3. Have the children complete their sheets.

✎ Activity 9

Aim: To let children respond verbally as to whether two words end with the same sound

Learning Outcome:

> Children can tell if two words end with the same sound.

Materials:
Fig. 41—Game board
Fig. 45—Word List 3
Fig. 47—Picture sheet
Fig. 51—Word List 4
Markers for game board

Method:

1. Say two words from Fig. 45. Ask the children, "*Do these two words end with the same sound?*" Children answer.

2. Repeat endings with Fig. 47 pictures.

3. Play the same game as in Activity 4, using words from Fig. 51.

Word List 4—Endings (Auditory) Fig. 51

snake	bell	street	crab
lock	well	seat	crib
clock	tell	meat	bib
quick	sell	cheat	cab
lick	quarrel	heat	sob
tick	will	put	rob
tock	mill	sat	
make	pull	fat	
take		bit	
		pit	

(*Continues on next page*)

sip	grass	bed	pan
pip	pass	said	man
tip	yes	red	men
top	guess	rid	pen
pop	less	rod	when
cap	mess	nod	then
nap	miss	mad	thin
lap	kiss	could	win
cup	cross	should	one
ship	loss	would	bun
		lid	
		kid	

Activity 10

Aim: To let children respond verbally as to whether the names of two of three pictures begin with the same sound

Learning Outcome:

> Children will name the pictures which begin with the same sound.

Materials: Fig. 52—Picture sheet, one copy per child
Crayons

Method:
1. Review the names of the pictures in Fig. 52. Point to the first row of pictures. Name the pictures. Ask, *"Which two pictures have the same beginning sound?"* Practice with all the sets in Fig. 52.

2. Model for the children how to color in the two pictures in each row of Fig. 52 that begin with the same sound.

3. Hand out copies of Fig. 52 and let the children complete their sheets.

✎ Activity 11

Aim: To let children respond verbally as to whether the names of two of three pictures end with the same sound

Learning Outcome:

> Children will name the pictures which end with the same sound.

Materials: Fig. 53—Picture sheet, one copy per child
Crayons

Method:
1. Review the names of the pictures in Fig. 53. Point to the first row of pictures. Name the pictures. Ask, *"Which two pictures have the same ending sound?"* Practice with all the sets in Fig. 53.

2. Model for the children how to color in the two pictures in each row of Fig. 53 that end with the same sound.

3. Hand out copies of Fig. 53 and let the children complete their sheets.

Figure 37

Word List 1

robin

rose

ride

rhyme

ravioli

rot

rat

rip

run

ribbon

Figure 38

Figure 39

Figure 40

Word List 2

ring	rhyme	fish	figure
road	rid	fan	funny
rock	ride	fun	fist
robin	rut	from	for
rose	ravioli	Frank	fig
man	Mike	sun	saddle
money	middle	soap	sorry
most	mouse	sad	sick
mud	mint	sack	sing
mist	motorcycle	soon	set
pen	pond		
pig	parrot		
penny	pencil		
picture	people		
pole	park		

Figure 41

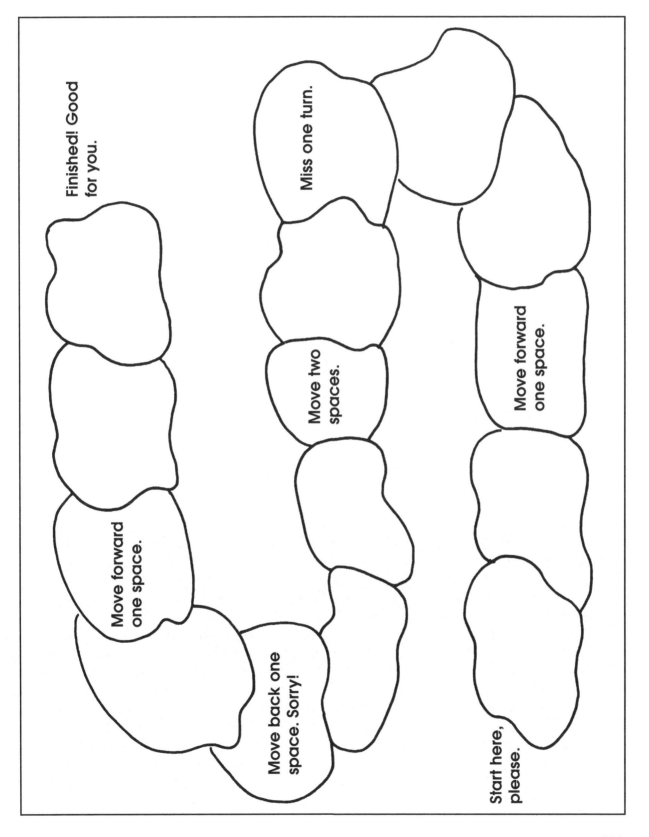

Finished! Good for you.

Miss one turn.

Move two spaces.

Move forward one space.

Move forward one space.

Move back one space. Sorry!

Start here, please.

Figure 42

Figure 43

Figure 44

Figure 45

Word List 3

street	put
seat	sat
meat	fat
cheat	bit
heat	pit

Figure 46

Figure 47

Figure 48

Figure 49

Figure 50

Figure 51

Word List 4—Endings (Auditory)

snake	bell	street	crab
lock	well	seat	crib
clock	tell	meat	bib
quick	sell	cheat	cab
lick	quarrel	heat	sob
tick	will	put	rob
tock	mill	sat	
make	pull	fat	
take		bit	
		pit	

sip	grass	bed	pan
pip	pass	said	man
tip	yes	red	men
top	guess	rid	pen
pop	less	rod	when
cap	mess	nod	then
nap	miss	mad	thin
lap	kiss	could	win
cup	cross	should	one
ship	loss	would	bun
		lid	
		kid	

Figure 52

Figure 53

PRONUNCIATION LESSONS ON CONSONANT PAIRS

Activity 1

Aim: To teach and improve the mouth positions required to produce consonants

Learning Outcome:

Children can pronounce *p* and *b*.

Materials: Mirror (use to observe mouth positions)

Methods:
1. Say, *"Put your lips together; don't let any air out yet. Now suddenly make the sound like a popping sound and let the air out."*

2. Say /**p**/. Say /**b**/. *"Do it with me. Feel the air on your hands."*

3. *"Say these words and feel the sound on your lips:"*

pen	banana
play	boat
plain	bat
peep	baby
pan	bench
pump	bank

(Continues on next page)

"Here are some words with p and b at the end:"

pup	crab
nap	grab
cap	club
sap	rub
cup	
help	
ship	

✎ Activity 2

Aim: To teach and improve the mouth positions required to produce consonants

Learning Outcome:

Children can pronounce *t* and *d*.

Materials: Mirror (use to observe mouth positions)

Method:

1. Say, *"Feel your tongue on the back of your two front teeth; feel the top of your tongue as you say /**t**/."* Do the same for /**d**/."

2. Say /**t**/; Say /**d**/.

3. *"Say these words and feel your tongue on the back of your two front teeth:"*

top	dad
tape	dog
tip	dinner
tennis	disk
television	day
tot	duck

"Here are some words with **t** *and* **d** *at the end:"*

tot	dad
bit	food
cat	bad
sat	sad
chat	wood
	good

Activity 3

Aim: To teach and improve the mouth positions required to produce consonants

Learning Outcome: Children can pronounce *k* and *g*.

Materials: Mirror (use to observe mouth positions)

Method:
1. Say, *"We are going to make a scraping sound in the back of our mouth. Watch what I do. Do it with me."*

2. Say /**k**/. Say /**g**/. *"What is happening to your tongue?"*

3. *"Say these words and feel the scraping sound in the back of your mouth:"*

king	good
kiss	game
kind	give
kit	gate
key	get

"Here are some words with **k** *and* **g** *at the end"*:

tick	gag
tack	flag
took	tag
clock	lag
ask	wag

✏ Activity 4

Aim: To teach and improve the mouth positions required to produce consonants

Learning Outcome:

> Children can pronounce *f* and *v*.

Materials: Mirror (use to observe mouth positions)

Method:

1. Say, "*Rest your top teeth on your bottom lip and blow. Put your hand in front of your mouth and feel it.*"

2. Say /*f*/. Say /*v*/. "*What do you feel?*"

3. "*Say these words and feel the sound on your lips*":

fit	van
full	voice
frog	violin
friend	visitor
fancy	vet

"*Here are some words with* **f** *and* **v** *at the end*":

staff	live
whiff	give
cliff	save
beef	wave
chief	behave

Activity 5

Aim:	To teach and improve the mouth positions required to produce consonants

Learning Outcome:

> Children can pronounce *th* and *th* (soft and hard).

Materials: Mirror (use to observe mouth positions)

Method:

1. Say, "*Let the tip of your tongue touch your top teeth. Watch as I do it. Do it with me. Put your hand in front of your mouth and listen to the sound.*"

2. Say /**th**/ (soft). Say /**th**/ (hard).

3. "*Say these words and feel the sound on your lips*":

the	thin
them	thank
their	three
then	thought
they	third
this	thimble
that	thistle
those	

"*Here are some words with soft* **th** *and hard* **th** *at the end*":

with	south
	mouth

✏ Activity 6

Aim:	To teach and improve the mouth positions required to produce consonants

Learning Outcome:	Children can pronounce *s* and *z*.

Materials: Mirror (use to observe mouth positions)

Method:

1. Say /s/. "*Let's make a snake sound. Watch as I do it.*"
2. "*Now let's do it together. Listen to the sound.*"
3. "*Let's make a zinging sound. Watch as I do it.*"
4. Say /z/. "*Now let's do it together. Listen to the sound.*"
5. "*Say these words*":

sat	zoo
sing	zebra
so	zap
soap	zipper
sausage	zone

"*Here are some words with* **s** *and* **z** *at the end*":

tops	fizz
glass	whiz
kiss	quiz
floss	jazz
cross	crazy

✎ Activity 7

Aim: To teach and improve the mouth positions required to produce consonants

Learning Outcome: Children can pronounce *ch* and j.

Materials: Mirror (use to observe mouth positions)

Method:
1. Say, "*Let's make a chopping sound. Listen and watch while I do it.*"

2. Say /**ch**/. "*Feel your jaw while we do it together.*"

3. "*Let's make a jumping sound. It's from deeper in your throat. Listen and watch while I do it.*"

4. Say /**j**/. "*Feel your throat while we do it together.*"

5. "*Say these words*":

chin	Jill
chip	Jack
chair	just
china	jump
chili	jelly
chew	jet

"*Here are some words with **ch** at the end*":

church

such

much

witch

Activity 8

Aim: To teach and improve the mouth positions required to produce consonants

Learning Outcome:

Children can pronounce *sh* and *zh*.

Materials: Mirror (use to observe mouth positions)

Method:
1. Say, "*Put your finger in front of your lips and do what I do. Watch as I do it.*"

2. Say /**sh**/. Say /**zh**/. "*Now let's do it together. Listen to the sound.*"

3. "*Say these words*":

    ship

    shall

    shell

    she

    sheep

    shoe

    "*Here are some words with* **sh** *at the end*":

    push

    crush

    woosh

    leash

BLENDING THE INDIVIDUAL PHONEMES

✏ Activity 1

Aim: To teach children the concept of blending individual phonemes together

Learning Outcome:

> Children will be aware of words being made up of individual phonemes.

Materials: Fig. 54—Car
Fig. 55—Man
Fig. 56—Train
Hand puppet

Method:

1. Say, *"Do you remember how Percy the Puppet spoke in a bumpy way? He said, '/c/—/at/' for* **cat**. *Now he is going to say, '/c/—/ar/' for* **car**. *See this car can break up into pieces."* Cut Fig. 54 in two. *"What does it say?* **Car.**

2. Say, *"Percy the Puppet can speak in an even more bumpy way. Let's listen to how he says this picture: /m/—/a/—/n/. What did he say? He said* **man**. *We can break* **man** *into three parts like this."* Cut Fig. 55 into three parts.

3. *"Let's listen to how he says this picture: /t/—/r/—/ai/—/n/. What did he say?"* Cut Fig. 56 into four pieces.

4. *"Listen to other words that Percy the Puppet can say."* Say the words on the next page, broken into phonemes. *"What do you think Percy the Puppet said?"*

(Continues on next page)

Two Phonemes	Three Phonemes	Four Phonemes
cow	hat	flag
up	jam	band
two	tap	sent
four	hit	black
ice	ship	grape

✏ Activity 2

Aim: To let children blend phonemes together when presented one at a time

Learning Outcome:

> Children show by "moving and saying it" that they can blend two-phoneme words.

Materials: Figs. 57–62—Pictures (can be laminated)
Fig. 57—Cow, one copy per child
Two colored cubes per child
Hand puppet

Method:
1. Say, "*When Percy the Puppet says a word we will move our cubes into the boxes to show the number of bumpy sounds in the word. Let's do the first one together. Percy says /c/ow/.*" Show how to move the cubes to match the phonemes in *cow*.

2. Say, "*Let's practice. Percy the Puppet says /c/ow/. Move your cubes to show /c/ow/.*"

3. Practice using all the pictures. Each child has a turn using a different picture.

List of Picture Words
(two phonemes) with boxes

cow

arm

zoo

two

four

car

🖉 Activity 3

Aim:	To let children blend phonemes together when presented one at a time

Learning Outcome:

> Children show by "moving and saying it" that they can blend three-phoneme words.

Materials: Figs. 63–68—Pictures (can be laminated)
Fig. 63—Ship, one copy per child
Three colored cubes per child
Hand puppet

Method:

1. Say, "*When Percy the Puppet says a word we will move our cubes into the boxes to show the number of bumpy sounds in the word. Let's do the first one together. Percy says /sh/i/p/.*" Show how to move the cubes to match the phonemes in *ship*.

2. Say, "*Let's practice. Percy the Puppet says /sh/i/p/. Move your cubes to show /sh/i/p/.*"

3. Practice using all the pictures. Each child has a turn using a different picture.

List of Picture Words
(three phonemes) with boxes

ship

leaf

sun

star

cat

dog

✎ Activity 4

Aim: To let children blend phonemes together when presented one at a time

Learning Outcome:

> Children show by "moving and saying it" that they can blend four-phoneme words.

Materials: Figs. 69–74—Pictures (can be laminated)
Fig. 69—Nest, one copy per child
Four colored cubes per child
Hand puppet

Method:

1. Say, "*When Percy the Puppet says a word we will move our cubes into the boxes to show the number of bumpy sounds in the word. Let's do the first one together. Percy says /n/e/s/t/.*" Show how to move the cubes to match the phonemes in *nest*.

2. Say, "*Let's practice. Percy the Puppet says /n/e/s/t/. Move your cubes to show /n/e/s/t/.*"

3. Practice using all the pictures. Each child has a turn using a different picture.

List of Picture Words
(four phonemes) with boxes

nest

clock

cats

crab

train

plane

Activity 5

Aim:	To let children show knowledge of the concept of blending two- and three-phoneme words

Learning Outcome:

> Children will show more consolidated awareness of how to blend two- and three-phoneme words.

Materials: Fig. 75—Word list of two- and three-phoneme words
Fig. 76—Grids (laminate one copy per child)
Five colored cubes
Hand puppet

Method:

1. Give out Fig. 76 and cubes to each child.

2. Say, "*Percy the Puppet will say a word. Listen carefully and move the cubes into the right boxes. Let's practice. Percy the Puppet says /z/oo/. Move your cubes. Which box will we choose? Will it be two boxes or three boxes?*"

3. "*Now Percy says /d/o/g/. Which box will we choose? Move your cubes. Will it be two boxes or three boxes?*"

4. Practice using the words in Fig. 75.

Two Phonemes	**Three Phonemes**
zoo	dog
arm	ship
cow	star
two	sun
four	leaf
car	cat

Figure 54

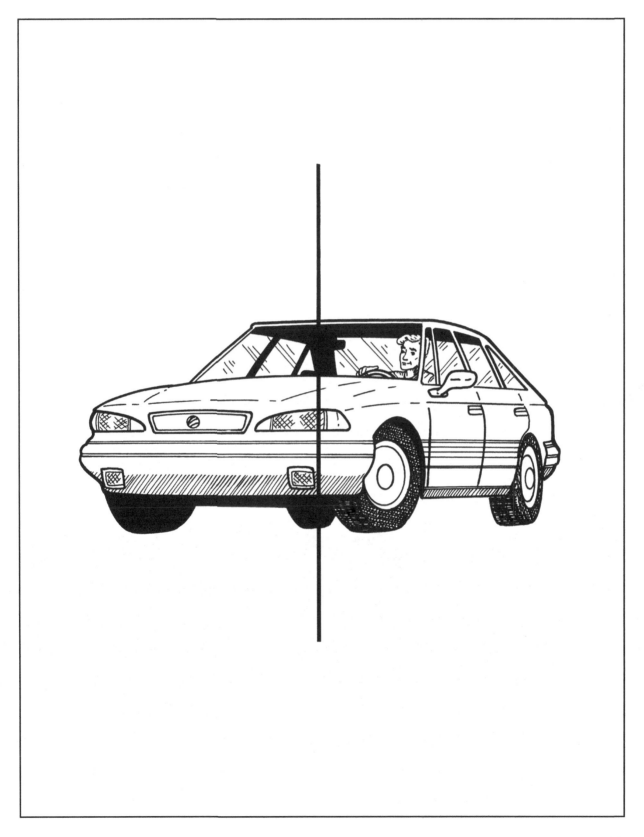

Figure 55

Figure 56

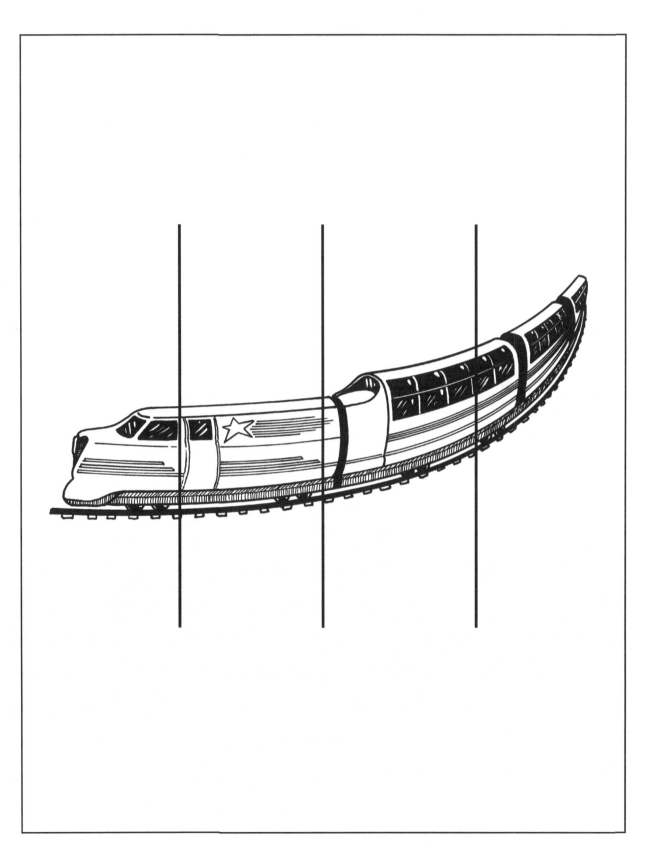

Figure 57

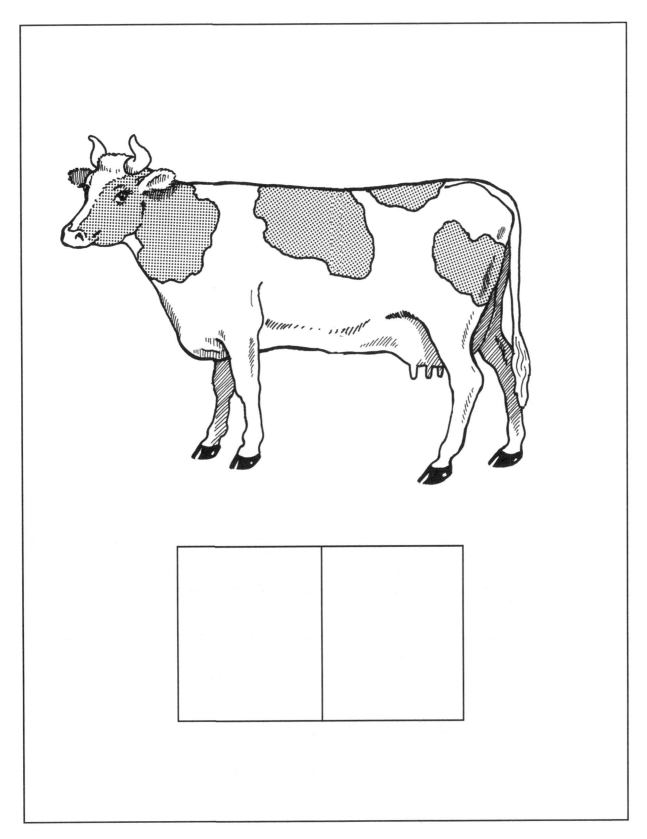

Figure 58

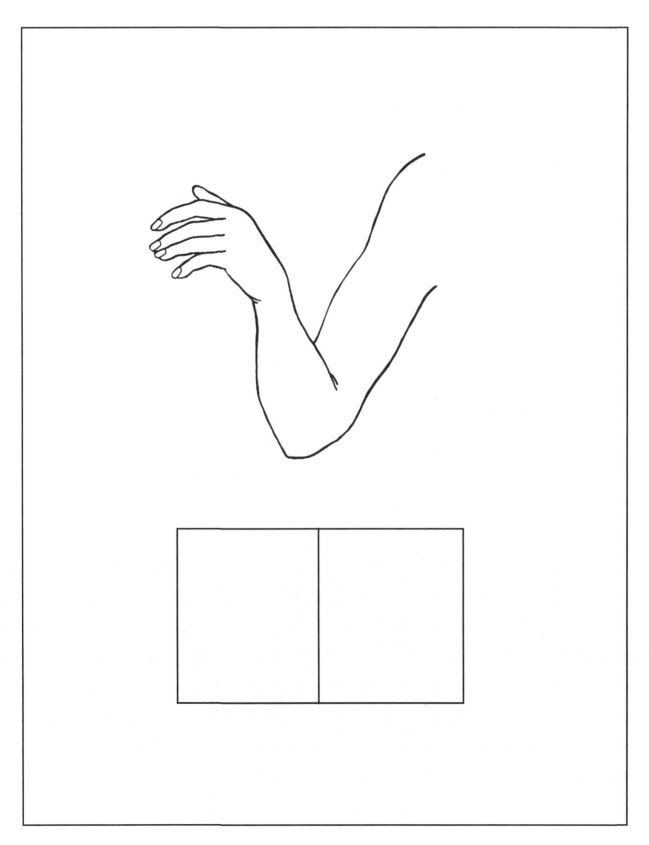

Figure 59

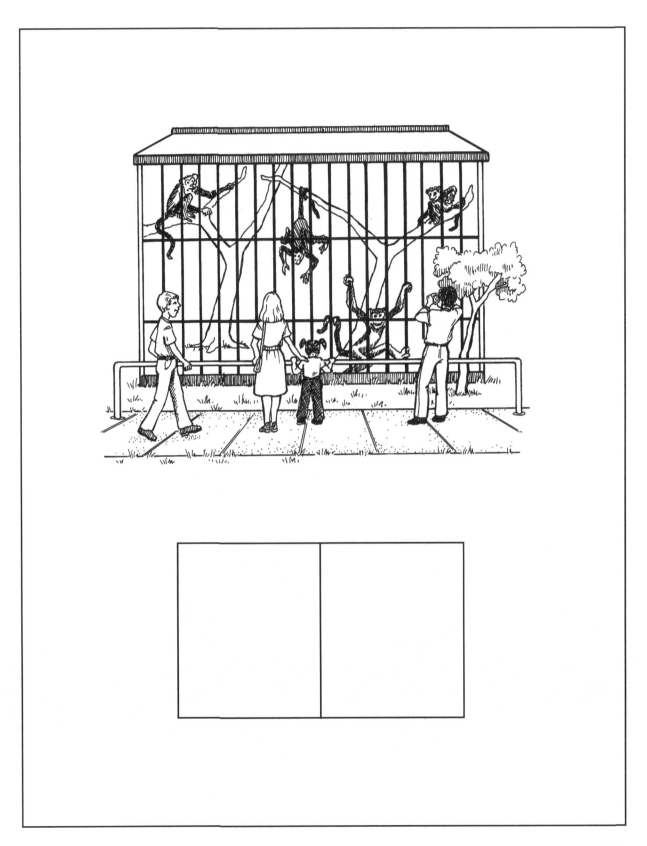

Figure 60

Figure 61

Figure 62

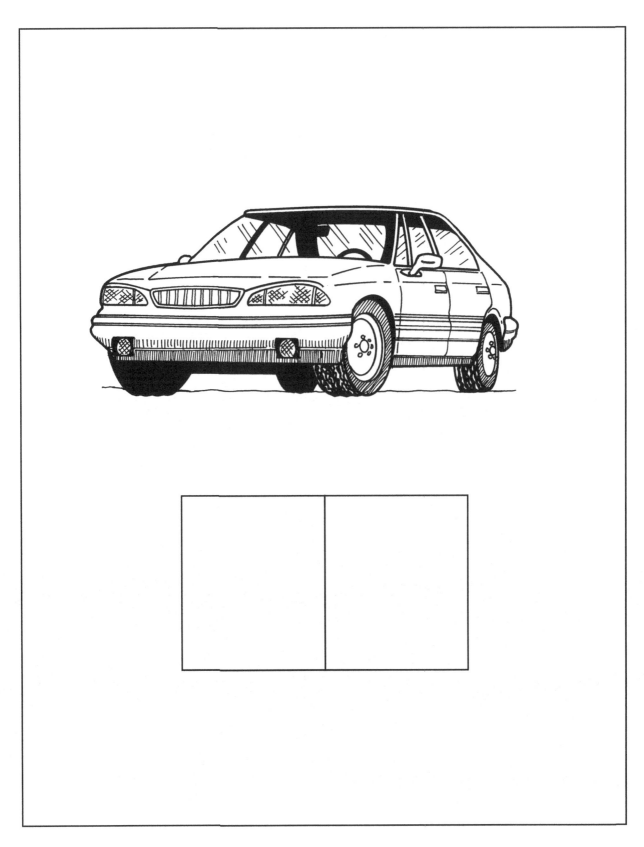

Figure 63

Figure 64

Figure 65

Figure 66

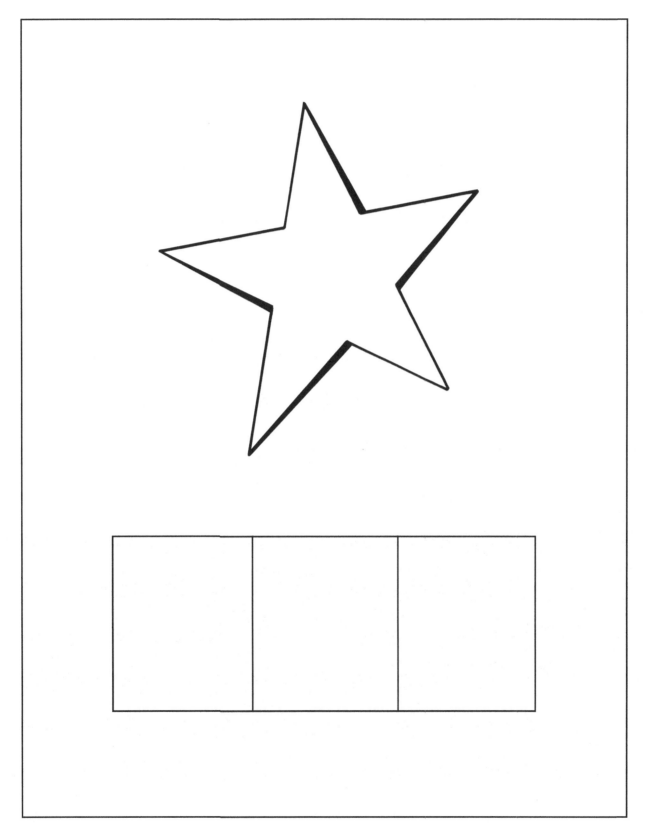

Figure 67

Figure 68

Figure 69

Figure 70

Figure 71

Figure 72

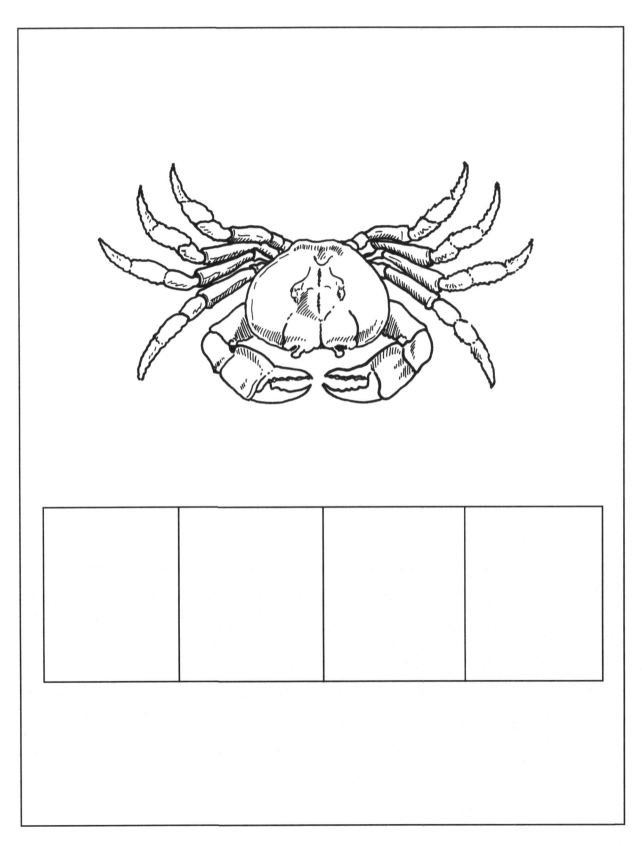

Figure 73

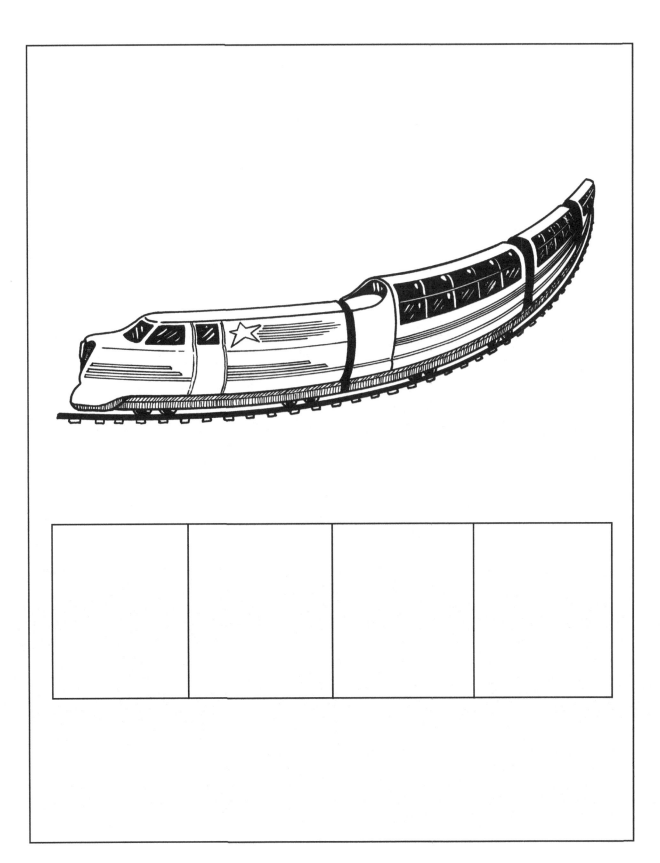

Figure 74

Figure 75

Two Phonemes

zoo

arm

cow

two

four

car

Three Phonemes

dog

ship

star

sun

leaf

cat

Figure 76

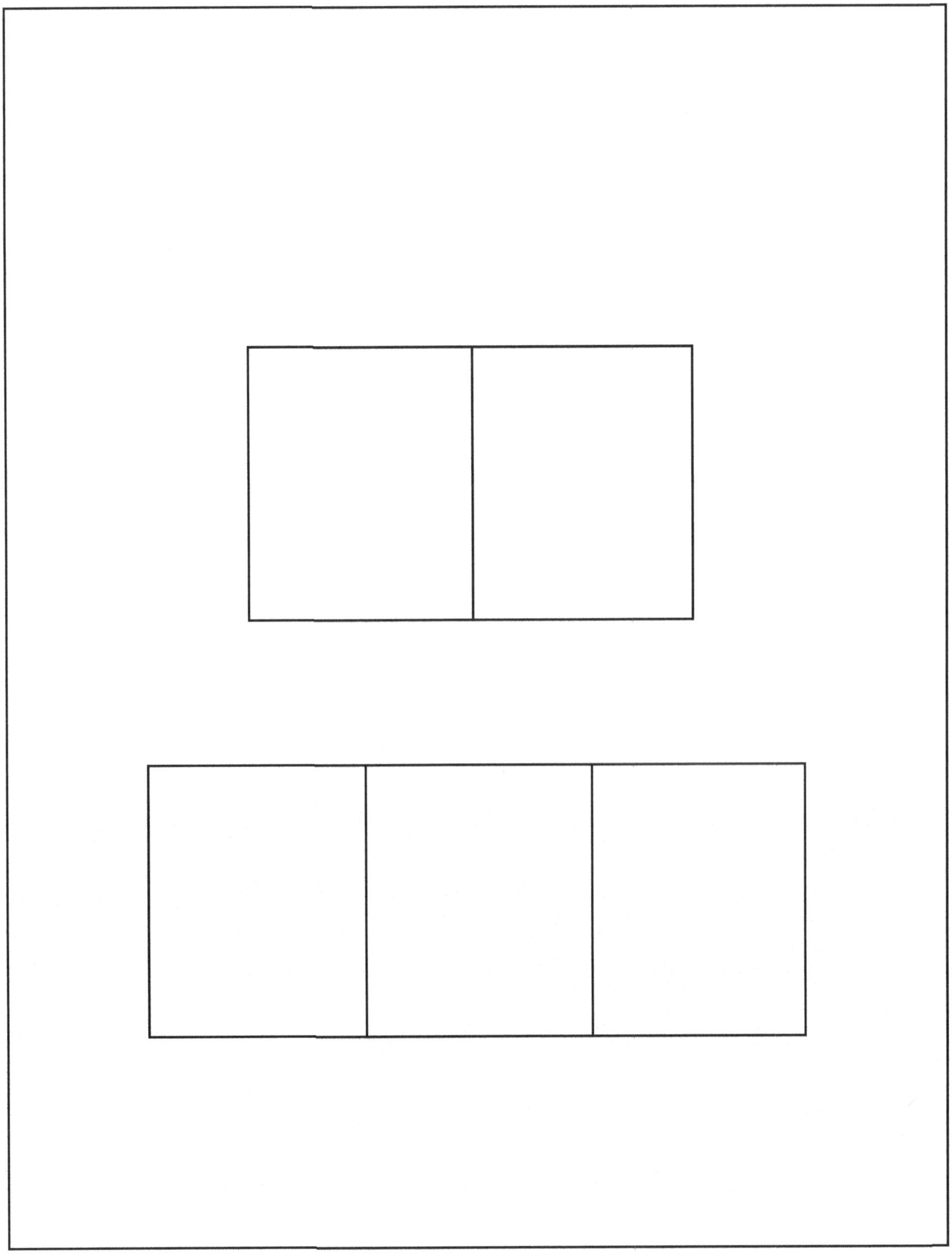

LINKAGE

✏ Activity 1

Aim: To let the children trace and say the sounds of a group of letters (**a p t m i**)

Learning Outcome:

> Children will spontaneously find, trace, and say the sounds of a group of letters (**a p t m i**).

Materials: Five plastic letters (**a p t m i**)
Fig. 77—Rainbow chart
Sand tray

Method:

1. Place letter *a* on Fig. 77. Point to letter *a* on the rainbow and say, "*This letter says* **a**. *You say* **a**." Child repeats sound. "*Watch me trace the shape of the letter starting here. It's* **a**. *You do that.*" Child copies.

2. Get the sand tray. "*Now I'll write it in the sand—***a**. *You do that, too.*" Child copies and says, "*a*," using sand tray. "*Well done. Now let's get the letter from the rainbow and trace it again.*"

3. Positive prompts are vital. In other words, avoid all negative statements, such as "*No, that's wrong*" or "*Not like that.*" Instead use:
    "*Let me show you that again.*"
    "*Let me see* **you** *try that again.*"
    "*Well done, that's much better than yesterday.*"
    "*Watch me again. Now you try.*"

✎ Activity 2

Aim: To let the children trace and say the sounds of a group of letters (**a p t m i**)

Learning Outcome:

> Children will spontaneously find, trace, and say the sounds of a group of letters (**a p t m i**).

Materials: Five plastic letters (**a p t m i**)
Fig. 77—Rainbow chart
Sand tray

Method:

1. Place letter *p* on Fig. 77. Point to letter *p* on the rainbow and say, "*This letter says* **p**. *You say* **p**." Child repeats sound. "*Watch me trace the shape of the letter starting here. It's* **p**. *You do that.*" Child copies.

2. Get the sand tray. "*Now I'll write it in the sand—***p**. *You do that, too.*" Child copies and says, "*p*," using sand tray. "*Well done. Now let's get the letter from the rainbow and trace it again.*"

3. As in Activity 1, positive prompts are vital.

✏ Activity 3

Aim: To let the children trace and say the sounds of a group of letters (**a p t m i**)

Learning Outcome:

> Children will spontaneously find, trace, and say the sounds of a group of letters (**a p t m i**).

Materials: Five plastic letters (**a p t m i**)
Fig. 77—Rainbow chart
Sand tray

Method:

1. Place letter *t* on Fig. 77. Point to letter *t* on the rainbow and say, "*This letter says* **t**. *You say* **t**." Child repeats sound. "*Watch me trace the shape of the letter starting here. It's* **t**. *You do that.*" Child copies.

2. Get the sand tray. "*Now I'll write it in the sand—***t**. *You do that, too.*" Child copies and says, "t," using sand tray. "*Well done. Now let's get the letter from the rainbow and trace it again.*"

3. As in Activity 1, positive prompts are vital.

Activity 4

Aim: To let the children trace and say the sounds of a group of letters (**a p t m i**)

Learning Outcome:

> Children will spontaneously find, trace, and say the sounds of a group of letters (**a p t m i**).

Materials: Five plastic letters (**a p t m i**)
Fig. 77—Rainbow chart
Sand tray

Method:

1. Place letter *m* on Fig. 77. Point to letter *m* on the rainbow and say, *"This letter says* **m**. *You say* **m**.*"* Child repeats sound. *"Watch me trace the shape of the letter starting here. It's* **m**. *You do that."* Child copies.

2. Get the sand tray. *"Now I'll write it in the sand—***m**. *You do that, too."* Child copies and says, *"m,"* using sand tray. *"Well done. Now let's get the letter from the rainbow and trace it again."*

3. As in Activity 1, positive prompts are vital.

✎ Activity 5

Aim: To let the children trace and say the sounds of a group of letters (**a p t m i**)

Learning Outcome:
> Children will spontaneously find, trace, and say the sounds of a group of letters (**a p t m i**).

Materials: Five plastic letters (**a p t m i**)
Fig. 77—Rainbow chart
Sand tray

Method:
1. Place letter *i* on Fig. 77. Point to letter *i* on the rainbow and say, "*This letter says* **i**. *You say* **i**." Child repeats sound. "*Watch me trace the shape of the letter starting here. It's* **i**. *You do that*." Child copies.

2. Get the sand tray. "*Now I'll write it in the sand—*i. *You do that, too*." Child copies and says, "*i*," using sand tray. "*Well done. Now let's get the letter from the rainbow and trace it again*."

3. As in Activity 1, positive prompts are vital.

✎ Activity 6

Aim: To help the children discriminate letter shapes within a discrete group of letters (**a p t m i**)

Learning Outcome:

> Children can match to a target letter fluently.

Materials: Figs. 78–81—Letter sheets, one copy of each page per child
Pencil or crayon for each child

Method:
1. Point to the first line of Fig. 78. Say, "*This letter is* **a**. *Now you see two more letters. Which letter is* **a**?"

2. Point to the second line of Fig. 78. Say, "*This letter is* **p**." Child responds, "**p**." "*Now you see two more letters. Which letter is* **p**?" Child points to respond. If incorrect, give correct feedback: "*That's not quite right. This letter is* **p**."

3. Now mark or circle the *a* and *p* with your pencil or crayon.

4. Check that the children know how to make a circle or mark.

5. Let the children complete letter sheets (Figs. 78–81)

✎ Activity 7

Aim: To help the children discriminate letter shapes within a discrete group of letters (**a p t m i**)

Learning Outcome:

> Children can match to a target letter fluently.

Materials: Figs. 82–83—Letter sheets, one copy of each page per child
Pencil or crayon for each child

Method:
1. Point to the first line of Fig. 82. Say, *"This letter is* **a***. Now you see three more letters. Which letter is* **a***?"*

2. Point to the second line of Fig. 82. Say, *"This letter is* ___*."* Child responds, *"***p***."* *"Now you see three more letters. Which letter is* **p***?"* Child points to respond. If incorrect, give correct feedback: *"That's not quite right. This letter is* **p***."*

3. Check that the children are still sure about how to circle the letters as they complete letter sheets (Figs. 82 and 83).

Activity 8

Aim: To help the children discriminate letter shapes within a discrete group of letters (**a p t m i**)

Learning Outcome:

Children can match to a target letter fluently.

Materials: Figs. 84–87—Letter sheets, one copy of each page per child
Pencil or crayon for each child

Method:
1. Point to the first line of Fig. 84. Say, *"This letter is* **p**. *Now you see four more letters. Which letter is* **p**?"

2. Point to the second line of Fig. 84. Say, *"This letter is* ___." Child responds, "**i**." *"Now you see four more letters. Which letter is* **i**?" If incorrect, give correct feedback: *"That's not quite right. This letter is* **i**."

3. Let the children complete their letter sheets (Figs. 84–87) by circling the correct letters with their pencils or crayons.

✏ Activity 9

Aim: To help the children discriminate letter shapes within a discrete group of letters (**a p t m i**)

Learning Outcome:

> Children can match to a target letter fluently.

Materials: Figs. 88–91—Letter sheets, one copy of each page per child
Pencil or crayon for each child

Method:

1. Point to the first line of Fig. 88. Say, "*This letter is* **a**. *Now you see five more letters. Which letter is* **a**?"

2. Point to the second line of Fig. 88. Say, "*This letter is* ___." Child responds, "**p**." "*Now you see five more letters. Which letter is* **p**?" If incorrect, give correct feedback: "*That's not quite right. This letter is* **p**."

3. Ask the children to respond by drawing a circle around the correct letter on each item of their sheets (Figs. 88–91).

✎ Activity 10

Aim: To work further on the relationship between letters and sounds and how letters are used to make words

Learning Outcome: Children will see and say letter symbols within whole, meaningful, three-letter words (using sound-symbol links with a printed word).

Materials: Fig. 92—Slide chart
Plastic letters (**a r p m t**)

Method:
1. Choose the plastic letter **a** and have the consonants ready. On Fig. 92, show how **r** can slide down and crash into "**am**" and "**ap**," making **ram** and **rap**.

2. Have the children say the words. If incorrect, say, "*That's not quite right. Watch and listen again.*" Then **p** can slide down and crash into "**at**" and "**am**." Then **m** can slide down and crash into "**at**" and "**ap**."

3. After modeling this with each of the consonants for the children as a group, repeat and let individual children say what the whole word is.

4. Again, if incorrect at any stage, model the correct word for the child.

✎ Activity 11

Aim: To work further on the relationship between letters and words and to include letter writing

Learning Outcome:

> Children will see and say letter symbols within whole, meaningful three-letter words and will print as they say.

Materials: Fig. 92—Slide chart
Fig. 93—Letter shapes sheet, one copy per child
Plastic letters (**m p t**)
Pencils

Method:

1. Use Fig. 92 and letters just as in Activity 10 to review the idea of sounds building into a word.

2. Give out a copy of Fig. 93 and pencil to each child.

3. Model the first item for the children. Say, "*Look at the letter* **m**. *Say* **m**. *Now look at the next box. With your pencil trace* **m**, *starting at the big dot.*" Check each individual child.

4. Let children complete sheet (Fig. 93).

Activity 12

Aim: To work further on the relationship between letters and sounds and how letters are used to make words

Learning Outcome:
> Children will see and say letter symbols within whole, meaningful, three-letter words (using sound-symbol links with a printed word).

Materials: Fig. 92—Slide chart
Plastic letters (**r p m i t**)

Method:
1. Introduce nonsense words. Choose the plastic letter **r** and have the other consonants ready. Show how **r** can slide down and crash into "**im**" and "**ip**," making **rim** and **rip**.

2. Have the children say the words. If incorrect, say, "*That's not quite right. Watch and listen again.*" Then **p** can slide down and crash into "**it**," and "**im**." Then **m** can slide down and crash into "**it**" and "**ip**."

3. After modeling this with each of the consonants for the children as a group, repeat and let individual children say what the whole word is.

4. Again, if incorrect at any stage, model the correct word for the child.

✏ Activity 13

Aim: To work further on the relationship between letters and words and to include letter writing

Learning Outcome:

> Children will see and say letter symbols within whole, meaningful, three-letter words and will print as they say.

Materials: Fig. 92—Slide chart
Fig. 94—Letter shapes sheet, one copy per child
Plastic letters (**p m t**)
Pencils

Method:
1. Use Fig. 92 and letters just as in Activity 10 to review the idea of sounds building into a word.

2. Give out a copy of Fig. 94 and pencil to each child.

3. Model the first item for the children. Say, "*Look at the letter* **p**. *Say* **p**. *Now look at the next box. With your pencil trace* **p**, *starting at the big dot.*" Check each individual child.

4. Let children complete sheet (Fig. 94).

🖉 Activity 14

Aim: To show children how their awareness of sounds in words is represented by letters of the alphabet

Learning Outcome:

Children can move letters to name the pictures in a "move it and say it" activity.

Materials: Figs. 95–99, Picture and word sheets
Fig. 77, Rainbow chart
Set of individual letters (**a m p t i**)

Method:

1. Show Figs. 95–99. Name the five pictures with the children (tap, mitt, pit, Tim, mat).

2. Show Fig. 99. Model how to move it and say it. Say, "/*m*/*at*/" as you move the letter *m* into the box next to "**at**" and say, "***mat***."

3. Show Fig. 77 with the plastic letters in the boxes. Show children how to choose letters to put next to the rime in the boxes in Figs. 95–99.

4. Give each child a turn to move it and say it. All the children in the group complete all the pictures in this way.

Figure 77

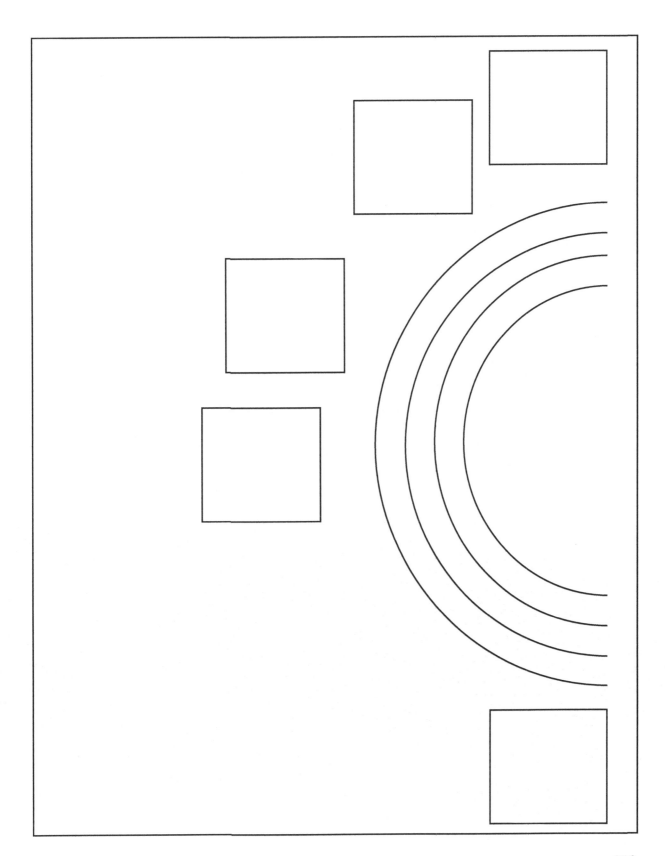

Figure 78

a	p	a
p	a	p
t	t	a
m	m	a
i	i	m
p	p	i

Figure 79

a	a	m
m	m	p
t	t	i
i	p	m
p	i	p
a	m	a

Figure 80

p	a	p
i	m	i
t	t	a
m	m	t
a	a	m
p	p	i

Figure 81

t	a	t
m	p	m
i	m	i
p	a	p
m	m	p
a	t	a

Figure 82

a	a	p	m
p	m	t	p
t	i	m	t
m	p	m	a
i	t	a	i
t	p	a	t

Figure 83

p	m	i	p
a	t	m	a
m	i	m	p
t	a	t	i
i	i	m	p
p	m	t	p

Figure 84

p	p	m	a	p
i	m	i	p	a
t	t	i	p	m
m	p	m	i	t
a	m	a	m	t
p	a	p	m	i

Figure 85

i	i	p	a	m
m	p	m	a	t
t	i	a	p	t
p	p	a	t	m
a	a	m	t	p

m	p	q	t	t
t	n	n	a	n
	p	c	i	t
m	t	p	q	q
q	t	m	p	q

Linkage

Figure 86

a	m	p	a	t
p	a	t	m	p
t	m	m	t	a
m	t	t	p	m
i	i	t	p	p
p	m	t	i	p

271

Figure 87

a	p	m	a	t
m	i	m	a	m
t	a	p	t	m
i	m	i	p	t
p	p	i	t	m

Linkage

Figure 88

a	p	i	m	a	t
p	t	a	p	i	m
t	i	a	t	m	p
m	t	i	p	m	a
i	p	a	m	t	i
t	i	a	t	m	p

275

Figure 89

p	p	i	m	t	a
a	i	a	m	p	t
m	p	t	a	i	m
t	m	a	p	t	i
i	p	i	a	t	m
p	m	t	p	i	a

Figure 90

a	m	a	p	t	a	i
p	i	t	p	a	p	m
t	i	a	m	t	a	t
m	t	i	m	p	m	a
i	p	m	i	t	m	i
t	i	a	t	m	t	p

Figure 91

p	p	i	p	m	t	a
a	i	a	m	a	p	t
m	m	t	p	a	i	m
t	m	a	p	t	t	i
i	i	p	a	m	i	m
p	m	t	p	a	p	i

Figure 92

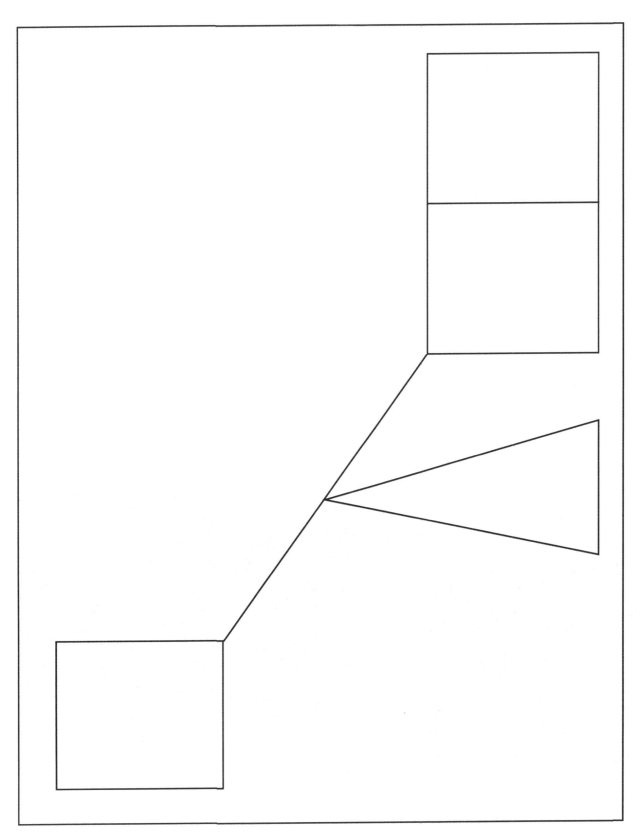

Figure 93

m	m⋅	__	__at	mat
p	p⋅	__	__at	pat
t	t⋅	__	__ap	tap
m	m⋅	__	__ap	map
P	P⋅	__	__am	Pam
t	t⋅	__	__am	tam

Figure 94

p	p	__	__it	pit
m	m	__	__it	mitt
t	t	__	__ip	tip
T	T	__	__im	Tim
m	m	__	__ip	mip
P	P	__	__im	Pim

Figure 95

a p

Figure 96

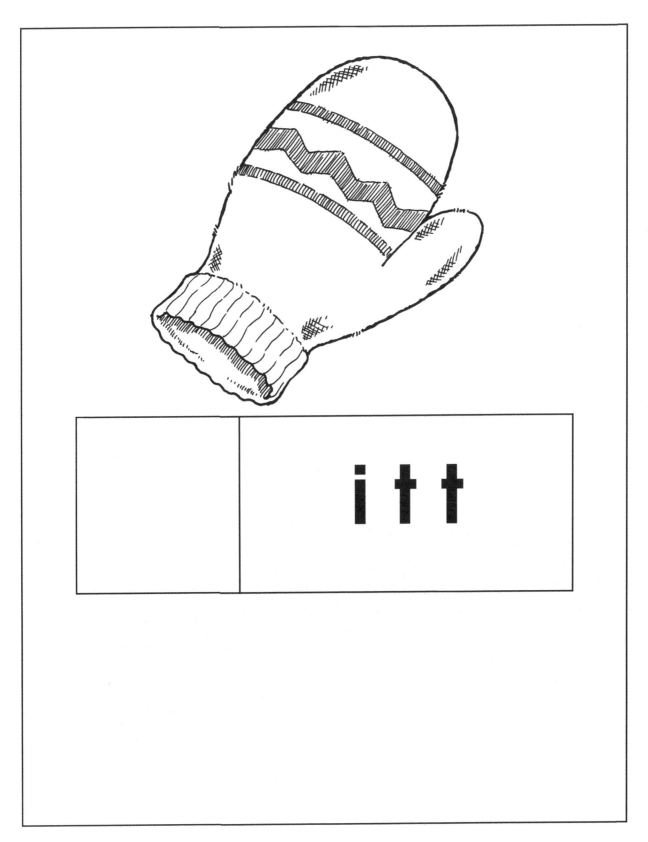

Figure 97

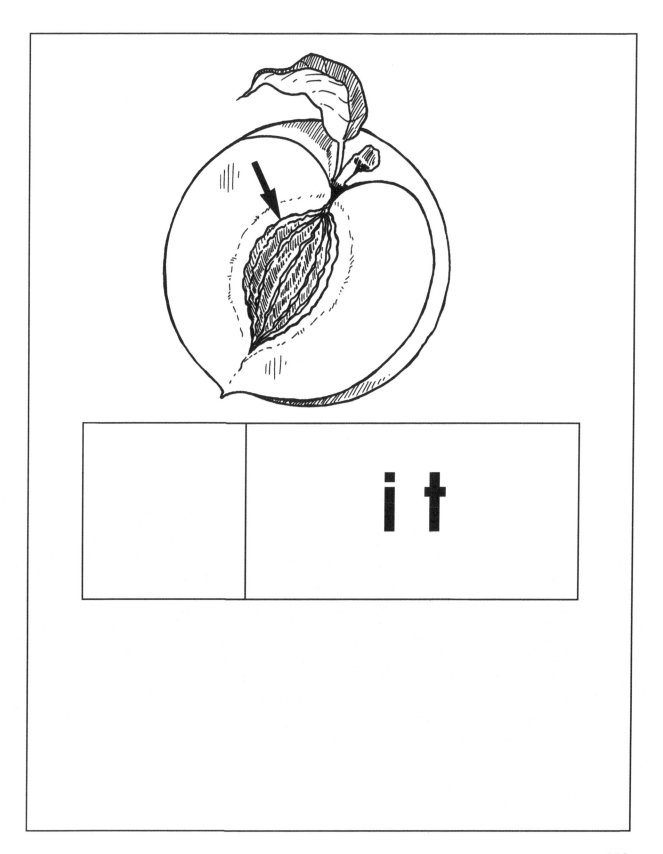

i t

Figure 98

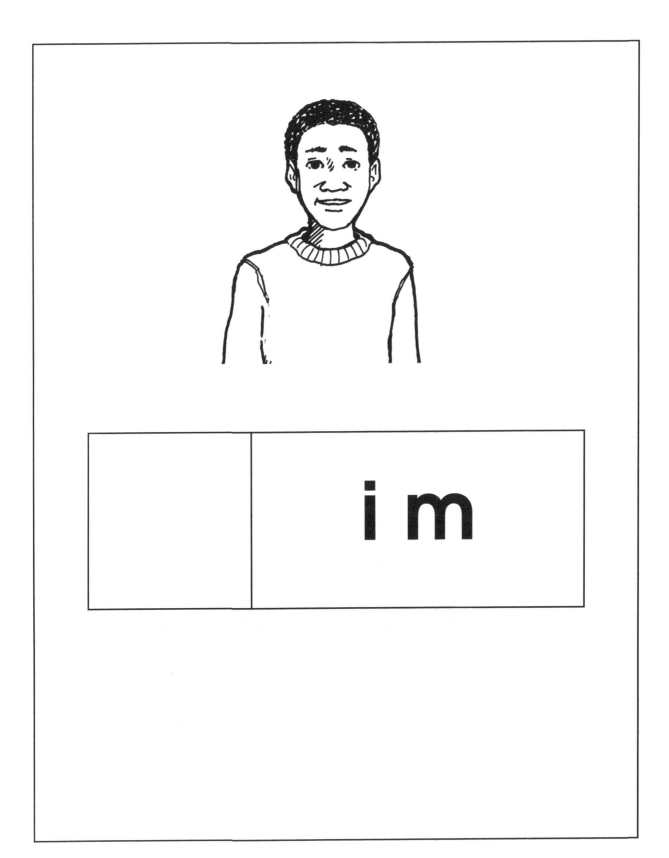

i m

Figure 99

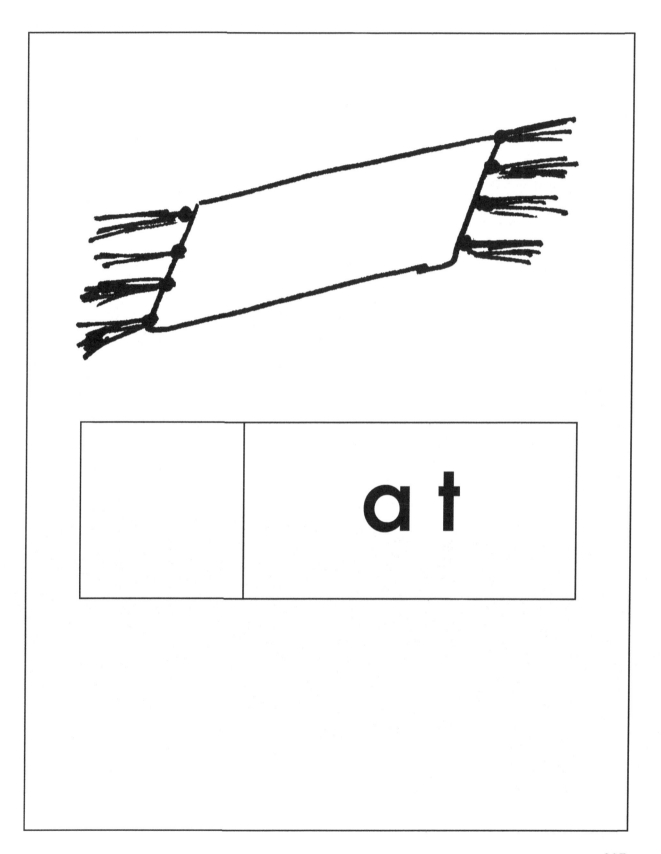

a t

BIBLIOGRAPHY

Adams, M. J. (1990). *Beginning to read. Thinking and learning about print.* Cambridge, MA: Massachusetts Institute of Technology Press.

Adams, M. J. , & Henry, M. K. (1997). Myths and realities about words and literacy. *School Psychology Review, 26*, 425–436.

Ball, E. W., & Blachman, B. A. (1991). Does phoneme awareness training in kindergarten make a difference in early word recognition and developmental spelling? *Reading Research Quarterly, 26*, 49–66.

Blachman, B. A. (1991). Early intervention for children's reading problems: Clinical applications of the research in phonological awareness. *Topics in Language Disorders, 12*, 51–65.

Blachman, B. A. (1994). What we have learned from longitudinal studies of phonological processing and reading, and some unanswered questions: A response to Torgesen, Wagner, and Rashotte. *Journal of Learning Disabilities, 27*, 287–291.

Blachman, B. A. (Ed.). (1997). *Foundations of reading acquisition and dyslexia: Implications for early intervention.* Hillsdale, NJ: Lawrence Erlbaum.

Bryant, P., & Bradley, L. (1985). *Children's reading problems.* Oxford, England: Blackwell.

Busink, R. (1997). Reading and phonological awareness: What we have learned and how we can use it. *Reading Research and Instruction, 36*, 199–215.

Byrne, B., & Fielding-Barnsley, R. (1993). Evaluation of a program to teach phoneme awareness to young children: A 1-year follow-up. *Journal of Educational Psychology, 85*, 104–111.

Catts, H., & Vartianinen, T. (1993). *Sounds abound.* Moline, IL: LinguiSystem, Inc.

Clay, M. (1991). *Becoming literate: The construction of inner control.* Portsmouth, NH: Heinemann.

Hatcher, P. (1994). *Sound linkage: An integrated program for overcoming reading difficulties.* London: Whurr.

Hatcher, P., Hulme, C., Ellis, A. W. (1994). Ameliorating early reading failure by integrating the teaching of reading and phonological skills: The phonological linkage hypothesis. *Child Development, 65*, 41–57.

Hulme, C., Muter, V., & Snowling, M. (1997). *Phonological Abilities Test.* London: Psychological Corporation.

Lindamood, C. H., & Lindamood, P. C. (1975). *Auditory discrimination in depth, Book 2.* Austin, TX: PRO-ED, Inc.

Morris, R. D., Stubing, K. K., Fletcher, J. M., Shaywitz, S. E., Lyon, G. R., Shankweiler, D. P., Katz, L., Francis, D. J., & Shawitz, B. A. (1998). Sub-types of reading disability: Variability around a phonological core. *Journal of Educational Psychology, 90*, 347–373.

Nicholson, R., & Fawcett, A. (1996). *The Dyslexia Early Screening Test.* London: The Psychological Corporation.

Research shows phonological awareness key to reading success. (1995). *CEC Today, 2*, 8–15.

Scanlon, D. M., & Vellutino, F. R. (1997). A comparison of the instructional backgrounds and cognitive profiles of poor, average, and good readers who were initially identified as at risk for reading failure. *Scientific Studies of Reading, 1*, 191–215.

Tangel, D. M., & Blachman, B. A. (1995). Effect of phoneme awareness instruction on the invented spelling of first-grade children: A one-year follow-up. *Journal of Reading Behavior, 27*, 153–167.

Torgesen, J. K., & Bryant, B. R. (1994a). *Phonological awareness training for reading.* Austin, TX: PRO-ED, Inc.

Torgesen, J. K., & Bryant, B. R. (1994b). *Test of Phonological Awareness.* Austin, TX: PRO-ED, Inc.

Torgesen, J. K., Wagner, R. K., & Rashotte, C. A. (1994). Longitudinal studies of phonological processing and reading. *Journal of Learning Disabilities, 27*, 276–286.

Torgesen, J. K., Wagner, R. K., & Rashotte, C. A. (1997). Prevention and remediation of severe reading disabilities: Keeping the end in mind. *Scientific Studies of Reading, 1*, 217–234.

Torgesen, J. K. (in press a). Instruction interventions for children with reading disabilities. In S. Shapiro, D. Accardo, & C. Capute (Eds.), *Dyslexia: Its conceptualization, diagnosis and treatment.* Parkton, MD: York Press.

Torgesen, J. K. (in press b). Phonologically based reading disabilities: Toward a coherent theory of one kind of learning disability. In R. J. Sremberg & L. Spear-Swerling (Eds.), *Perspectives on learning disabilities*. Hillsdale, NJ: Lawrence Erlbaum.

Vandervelden, M. C., & Siegel, L. S. (1997). Teaching phonological processing skills in early literacy: A developmental approach. *Learning Disability Quarterly, 20,* 63–82.

Van Kleek, A. (1995). Emphasizing form and meaning separately. *Topics in Language Disorders, 16*(1), 27–49.

APPENDIX

STUDENT RECORD SHEETS

The record forms are extremely important. The whole idea of early intervention means that there will be children with mild, moderate, and severe difficulties in each group. Over the course of the intervention it is important to track their progress. Each child's rate of progress and unexpected difficulties will begin to show over time.

USE OF INDIVIDUAL RECORD SHEET

The form has the child's name, class, and date started. To know when the program started is very important, so that the dates learning was achieved give a record of how long the teaching took. The comments give details of problems that were observed.

For example, Stephen (see sample Student's Record Sheet) has had quite a lot of difficulty, even with the first session, where the concept of a word as a unit of sound was not clear. However, the Tapping section helped to consolidate his newly acquired awareness. The Rhyme section again challenged him, so that more time had to be spent on the later stages.

USE OF THE GROUP SUMMARY RECORD SHEET

Often the program may be implemented by a teacher aide or parent volunteer, under the supervision of the teacher. This form allows the teacher to have a summary of the performance of the group as a whole. At a glance, the teacher can make decisions about which children might need extra help at other times of the day.

There is also an example of how to complete the Group Summary Record Sheet.

Phonological Awareness Training
Student's Record Sheet

Name _____Stephen M._____   Class _____K_____

Date Started ___January 10th___

UNIT	ACTIVITY NUMBER	COMMENTS	DATE ACHIEVED
AWARENESS OF WHOLE WORDS	1 ☑ 3 ☑ 2 ☑ 4 ☑	Has difficulty with 1 word, 2 OK, 3 took a lot of practice.	Jan. 31st
TAPPING	1 ☑ 3 ☑ 2 ☑ 4 ☑	Did well. Reinforced awareness of words.	Feb. 8th
RHYME	1 ☐ 4 ☐ ⑦☐ 2 ☐ ⑤☐ ⑧☐ 3 ☐ ⑥☐	Understood concept. Could identify but got stuck on odd ones out and production.	Mar. 10th
ONSET AND RIME	1 ☐ 3 ☐ 5 ☐ 2 ☐ 4 ☐		
SEGMENTATION OF WORDS INTO SYLLABLES	1 ☐ 3 ☐ 5 ☐ 2 ☐ 4 ☐		
SEGMENTATION OF WORDS INTO PHONEMES	1 ☐ 2 ☐		
DISCRIMINATION	1 ☐ 5 ☐ 9 ☐ 2 ☐ 6 ☐ 10 ☐ 3 ☐ 7 ☐ 11 ☐ 4 ☐ 8 ☐		
BLENDING PHONEMES	1 ☐ 3 ☐ 5 ☐ 2 ☐ 4 ☐		
LINKAGE	1 ☐ 6 ☐ 11 ☐ 2 ☐ 7 ☐ 12 ☐ 3 ☐ 8 ☐ 13 ☐ 4 ☐ 9 ☐ 14 ☐ 5 ☐ 10 ☐		
PRONUNCIATION	p/b ☐ th/th ☐ t/d ☐ s/z ☐ k/g ☐ sh/zh ☐ f/v ☐ ch/j ☐		

Notes: ✓ = achieved
⃝ = some difficulty

Group Summary Record Sheet

AWARENESS OF WHOLE WORDS	Act.	Adam V.	Ben C.	Angela P.	Gloria E.	Peter S.	Sam G.							
Took 2 weeks –	1	✓	✓	✓	✓	✓	✓							
AV & BC had problems!	2	✓	✓	✓	✓	✓	✓							
	3	✓	✓	✓	✓	✓	✓							
	4	✓	✓	✓	✓	✓	✓							
TAPPING														
Took one week only!	1	✓	✓	✓	✓	✓	✓							
All managed fine.	2	✓	✓	✓	✓	✓	✓							
	3	✓	✓	✓	✓	✓	✓							
	4	✓	✓	✓	✓	✓	✓							
RHYME														
Everyone went smoothly	1	✓	✓	✓	✓	✓	✓							
at first.	2	✓	✓	✓	✓	✓	✓							
	3	✓	✓	✓	✓	✓	✓							
	4	✓	✓	✓	✓	✓	✓							
GE, AV, BC, PS	5	✓	✓	✓	✓	✓	✓							
took more time here.	6			✓	✓	✓	✓							
	7			✓			✓							
	8			✓			✓							
ONSET AND RIME														
	1													
	2													
	3													
	4													
	5													

Phonological Awareness Training

Student's Record Sheet

Name _____ Class _____

Date Started _____

UNIT	ACTIVITY NUMBER	COMMENTS	DATE ACHIEVED
AWARENESS OF WHOLE WORDS	1 ☐ 3 ☐ 2 ☐ 4 ☐		
TAPPING	1 ☐ 3 ☐ 2 ☐ 4 ☐		
RHYME	1 ☐ 4 ☐ 7 ☐ 2 ☐ 5 ☐ 8 ☐ 3 ☐ 6 ☐		
ONSET AND RIME	1 ☐ 3 ☐ 5 ☐ 2 ☐ 4 ☐		
SEGMENTATION OF WORDS INTO SYLLABLES	1 ☐ 3 ☐ 5 ☐ 2 ☐ 4 ☐		
SEGMENTATION OF WORDS INTO PHONEMES	1 ☐ 2 ☐		
DISCRIMINATION	1 ☐ 5 ☐ 9 ☐ 2 ☐ 6 ☐ 10 ☐ 3 ☐ 7 ☐ 11 ☐ 4 ☐ 8 ☐		
BLENDING PHONEMES	1 ☐ 3 ☐ 5 ☐ 2 ☐ 4 ☐		
LINKAGE	1 ☐ 6 ☐ 11 ☐ 2 ☐ 7 ☐ 12 ☐ 3 ☐ 8 ☐ 13 ☐ 4 ☐ 9 ☐ 14 ☐ 5 ☐ 10 ☐		
PRONUNCIATION	p/b ☐ th/<u>th</u> ☐ t/d ☐ s/z ☐ k/g ☐ sh/zh ☐ f/v ☐ ch/j ☐		

Notes: ✓ = achieved
        ◯ = some difficulty

Group Summary Record Sheet

Name of Student	Act.												
AWARENESS OF WHOLE WORDS	Act.												
	1												
	2												
	3												
	4												
TAPPING													
	1												
	2												
	3												
	4												
RHYME													
	1												
	2												
	3												
	4												
	5												
	6												
	7												
	8												
ONSET AND RIME													
	1												
	2												
	3												
	4												
	5												

(Continues on next page)

Group Summary Record Sheet

(Continued)

	Name of Student											
SEGMENTATION OF WORDS INTO SYLLABLES	Act.											
	1											
	2											
	3											
	4											
	5											
SEGMENTATION OF WORDS INTO PHONEMES												
	1											
	2											
DISCRIMINATION												
	1											
	2											
	3											
	4											
	5											
	6											
	7											
	8											
	9											
	10											
	11											
PRONUNCIATION												
	1											
	2											
	3											
	4											

(Continues on next page)

Group
Summary
Record Sheet
(Continued)

Name of Student														
PRONUNCIATION *(Continued)*	Act.													
	5													
	6													
	7													
	8													
BLENDING THE INDIVIDUAL PHONEMES														
	1													
	2													
	3													
	4													
	5													
LINKAGE														
	1													
	2													
	3													
	4													
	5													
	6													
	7													
	8													
	9													
	10													
	11													
	12													
	13													
	14													

ABOUT THE AUTHORS

Lorna Bennett

Lorna Bennett, PhD, has 30 years of experience teaching kindergarten through university. In 1986, Lorna was recognized by her colleagues with the David Kendall Master Teacher Award. As a teacher of teachers, she has conducted extensive professional training throughout British Columbia on program modification and the inclusion of learning disabled children. She is a member of the Reading/Language in Early Childhood Committee of the International Reading Association (1999–2000).

Lorna established a district-based Diagnostic Center and implemented ongoing support for children with learning problems.

Lorna has been a member of a Canadian team of teachers, sponsored by the British Columbia Teachers' Federation and the Canadian Teachers' Federation, to teach educators in Guyana (1991, 1999) and Thailand (1993).

Lorna is currently a school psychologist in School District 44 (North Vancouver).

Pamela Ottley

Pamela Ottley, Ph.D., is an educational psychologist who studied at University College, London, Brooks College, Oxford, and the University of British Columbia. She has many years of experience as a psychologist in the U.K. and Canada in both the public and private sectors.

Pam began to provide workshops on early screening and intervention in England before the first commercial tests were available. She also co-wrote an intervention program that became used throughout Hampshire schools. She continued to make presentations on this subject as both screening and intervention methods became more numerous and widely available: in the UK, the USA and Canada.

Currently Pam is an independent educational consultant, providing assessment and consultancy services to students, teachers and parents and also offering workshops and training for teachers and parents.

As well as being co-author of "Launch Into Reading Success: Through Phonological Awareness Training", she has written "Sound Track for Reading" (Vancouver CA: LEARNING SOLUTIONS).

Printed in the United States
By Bookmasters